Learning Through Child Observation

Mary Fawcett

Jessica Kingsley Publishers
London and Bristol, Pennsylvania

For Trevor with love

First published in the United Kingdom in 1996 by
Jessica Kingsley Publishers Ltd
116 Pentonville Road
London N1 9JB, England
and
1900 Frost Road, Suite 101
Bristol, PA 19007, U S A

Copyright © 1996 Mary Fawcett

Library of Congress Cataloging in Publication Data
A CIP catalogue record for this book is available from the Library of Congress

British Library Cataloguing in Publication Data
A CIP catalogue record for this book is available from the British Library

ISBN 1-85302-288-8

Printed and bound in Great Britain by
Athenæum Press Ltd, Gateshead, Tyne & Wear

Learning Through Child Observation

of related interest

Handbook of Theory for Practice Teachers in Social Work
Edited by Joyce Lishman
ISBN 1 85302 098 2

Competence in Social Work Practice
Edited by Kieran O'Hagan
ISBN 1 85302 332 9

Play Therapy
Where the Sky Meets the Underworld
Ann Cattanach
ISBN 1 85302 211 X

Six Theories of Child Development
Edited by Ross Vasta
ISBN 1 85302 137 7

Child Play
Its Importance for Human Development
Peter Slade
ISBN 1 85302 246 2

Chain Reaction
Children and Divorce
Ofra Ayalon and Adina Flasher
ISBN 1 85302 136 9

Contents

Acknowledgements

For more than twenty years, through contacts with students and colleagues in many different settings, my interest in the subject of observation has grown and deepened. It is almost invidious to single anyone out, but I must record my gratitude to Barbara Primmer (who first introduced me to child observation) and to Sonia Jackson for all her support and encouragement. Particular thanks are also due to several Bristol colleagues, Margaret Boushel, Mike Fisher, Tara Mistry and Julie Selwyn, as well as to Sue Phillips and other members of the CCETSW observation group in the South West, and finally to Sue Copping for preparing the charts and diagrams. Any failings in this book are of course my sole responsibility.

Introduction

Learning Through Child Observation is a handbook designed for anyone working or preparing to work with young children and their families in any kind of setting, whether in education/care, social work or health, in both the independent and the public sectors. Students of all ages, and their tutors, involved in NVQ, GCSE, BTEC, the Diploma in Social Work, BEd and other degree courses will find practical guidance here about how to set up and carry out observations. The observational study of children will be set in context in several different ways.

The first chapter looks at the reasons *Why Observation Matters*, and shows that all students can benefit from developing the skills and understanding associated with observation. The next chapter, *Changing Views of Child Observation*, offers a short overview of the history of child observation and contemporary views on some child development theories. The observer's ways of thinking about children and development are also considered here, as well as the way in which perceptions about such topics as culture and gender are influenced by our own upbringing, education and experiences. Looking at the context of observations in yet another way, Chapter Three describes some of the varied *Pre-school Settings* in which children are likely to be observed.

The subject of Chapter Four is *Observational Methods and Practice*. Several methods, their various strengths and limitations, and examples of each are set out. The aim of this chapter is to help students, workers or tutors in their selection of the most appropriate method for their task. In the last section of this chapter the evaluation of observational visits is examined: what impact these sessions may have had on all the participants, the children, the parents, the pre-school workers, and the observers themselves. Chapter Five is titled *Child Observations: Exploring Themes.* Here possible topics for study arising from observations are suggested – themes such as communication, attachment and play. *Observation as a Tool for Assessment* is the focus of Chapter Six. Co-operation and collaboration between staff in the various organisations and services for pre-school children, especially since the Children Act (1989), require an understanding of the different perspectives on key tasks such as assessment. Chapter Six attempts to unravel this important concept.

The final chapter, *Teaching Child Observation,* is particularly targeted at tutors planning course programmes which involve observation tasks. The needs of the Diploma in Social Work is given some priority, since this course has up to now lacked much material on planned observation.

Throughout the book two important principles are specially underlined. The first is the need to see children 'holistically' and as unique individuals, and to concentrate on what they *actually do and say.* The second is the significance of the ecological setting of each child's life: family, community, culture, economic situation, geographical location, and the wider influences which impact on their development.

Observation of children can be a fascinating, absorbing and revealing experience. As a tool for study it is richly interesting and almost always enjoyable. More than that, once the skills have been learned they are potentially useful across all work involving people, whatever their age or background.

CHAPTER ONE

Why Observation Matters

Observation is a skill almost anyone can develop. It is a kind of perceptive watching, an informed way of looking that raises awareness and sharpens understanding. It helps bring to notice what might otherwise be over-looked.

Of course people are 'perceiving' the world about them all the time. They must – for their own self-preservation. But what they take in is limited and selective. Imagine someone walking across a park in spring-time but failing to hear the birdsong; or noticing birds singing but without realising they have heard two blackbirds, a robin, a song thrush, and a wren; or recognising these birds but not understanding why they are singing in the first place. This person, we might say, is not fully tuned in to birds. Observation is a means of tuning in to children.

We all have a tendency to see what we are looking for and to look for only what we know about. Rarely do we take time to stop and watch intently. It is also easy to assume that other people notice what we notice, and that they necessarily interpret it in the same way. All of us have our own preconceptions, our particular mind-sets and prejudices. A few people are natural 'observers', but most of us have to learn how to do it effectively, how to focus systematically in a detached and open-minded manner on the subject of our observation. The skills of observation, once learned, have relevance and use in all kinds of situations and roles.

What observation teaches

Skilled observers gather information in a systematic, detailed and precise way while recognising their own inevitable subjectivity. Through practice they acquire the ability to concentrate with full attention. This means avoiding direct involvement in the situation: they learn how *to be* and not *to do*. Although it is possible to acquire such skills through practice alone, deeper understanding comes through structured learning, and notably through group discussion, study and reflection. The scope for learning afforded by observation is great and extends across various dimensions: practical skills, factual and theoretical knowledge, values and attitudes.

Among the practical skills which can be learned from observation are the ability to remain detached, to suspend judgement, and to refrain from participation. Preparation for observational sessions also teaches what recording methods and techniques are available, how to evaluate their strengths and limitations, and how to select the most suitable one for a particular task. The skills involved in setting up a series of observations responsibly are not insignificant, since they may include negotiation of the arrangement with staff and parents (including the sharing of information) and ensuring that the rights of the children and adults involved are respected. Students will learn how anti-discriminatory principles can be put into practice, how power and hierarchies operate, and especially how relatively power*less* children are in society. They will gain insight too into the effects of the observer's presence on the adults and children in the observational setting. Those new to working with children will learn the first stage in communicating with them. By discovering how to observe they begin to get a sense of 'where the children are', in other words the stage they have reached, the worlds they inhabit. This can be an empowering activity.

Observation provides a rewarding opportunity to discover the subtle and fascinating ways in which people communicate, both verbally and non-verbally, and about cultural differences in communication, for example the use of gestures, smiling, and eye-contact. In addition, observation clearly has much to teach with regard to child development in all its aspects: physical, social, emotional and cognitive. The observer learns how curious, sociable, and intensely active young children are in reality. Close observation may also reveal on occasion that the child being observed has some disability, developmental delay, or particular need, which has so far escaped detection. It can be especially valuable in helping students grasp the concept of a 'holistic' view of children – that is to say the belief that children are not only complex and unique individuals, but that the different strands of their development are inextricably bound up together and must all be taken into account.

Theories of child development may be put in context, critically evaluated, and then used as a tool to help explain or suggest possible progress of a particular child. One such theoretical framework suggests an 'ecological' view of each child as part of a family with its own circumstances, a family which in turn is located within a cultural group, a group which is also situated within a society at a particular moment in history. This broader view focuses attention on both the social and economic circumstances of families, and the effect of health and social policies laid down by central government and local authorities. Students engaged in planned observations should bear in mind this wider ecological context, as well as the narrower ecological context of the pre-school settings in which children often spend the greater part of their day.

All the same, observation is not purely a learning activity for students on courses. It is an essential skill for anyone working with children, in whatever capacity. The assessment of a child, for example, should always incorporate the findings of careful observation, which may provide fundamental data in deciding on further action – whether this means the planning of specific educational activities for the child, some form of intervention by the agency, or the seeking of specialist help. Regular observational studies can also be of great value in alerting staff to possible improvements in their day-to-day practice and their environment.

In the area of personal learning, observation may help to promote self-awareness. Students should be encouraged to recognise and examine their personal responses during observation, to reflect on the origin of such responses and, if necessary, deal with any dilemmas that arise. Within the student group comparisons of observations bring home to participants their own perceptions, as well as those of colleagues, and demonstrate how subjective reactions often are. In the same way professionals of different backgrounds often find mutual discussion of observational studies extremely revealing.

Child development and observation: national concerns

Nationally there are persuasive arguments for increasing the emphasis on child observation in various professional and para-professional training courses. In recent years other demanding priorities have tended to force the topic of child observation out of some courses, in particular the initial training of social workers and teachers. In the case of social work education there was previously a much stronger child development component. Now, as a broader, more generic programme has evolved, less and less time is being devoted to this topic. Contributing to the problem has been uncertainty as to the most appropriate style of teaching. The Tavistock model of child observation (Miller *et al.*, 1989), originally a strong influence on social work course programmes, is based on psycho-analytic theory. Here students spend an hour a week, for a whole year, observing infant–mother interaction within the home environment. While this is undoubtedly a valuable learning experience, the time commitment is usually impractical. Moreover, the focus is limited to one type of interaction, fails to take account of the ecological context, and concentrates primarily on the young infant and on attachment theories. Other difficulties, which simply compound the time problem, are the lack of teaching staff with appropriate experience and the dearth of suitable textbooks.

There does seem to be a movement, however, towards re-establishing child observation. CCETSW (Central Council for Education and Training in Social Work, 1991) identified observation as a core skill in the Diploma in Social Work (DipSW). Various articles (Trowell and Miles, 1991; Wilson, 1992; and McMahon and Farnfield, 1994) give accounts of child observation in DipSW course programmes, though these are all to some extent based on the 'Tavistock model', and Baldwin (1994) has subjected some of the issues to careful scrutiny, especially the problems of power and rights. CCETSW has encouraged various initiatives – among them a pilot project in the South West of England (see Chapter Seven).

This fresh impetus stems to a large extent from the recognition that, in some recent tragic cases of child abuse or death, social work staff were insufficiently perceptive about the children involved and even lacked understanding of their physical condition. The report of the Cleveland affair poignantly reminded us that every child must be seen above all as 'a person and not an object of concern'. Similarly, in his review of child death inquiries for the Department of Health, Noyes (1991) highlights the need for greater awareness of the very existence of the child. It seems that in very stressful circumstances social workers tend to pay more attention to the adults than to the children. Department of Health guidance for social workers on making assessments (Phillips, 1988) states that they must listen carefully to what children are saying, must understand the cultural and religious background, be able to record carefully, know about child development, and be aware of their own values and prejudices. Too often, Phillips notes, social workers engaged in child protection do not pay sufficient attention to '*what is actually happening to the child*' (his italics, p.32).

In the case of teacher education, which has now become primarily concerned with preparing teachers for the National Curriculum, the concentration on specific curriculum subjects and the testing of children over five years of age dominate. Child development has thus been downgraded. It is now a minor topic, while even pedagogy (how to teach) has almost disappeared from training courses. Furthermore, the study of children under five is now very rare indeed in teacher education. The result must be that new generations of teachers will know less and less of young children, how they develop and learn. Yet there is perhaps some hope for a change in attitudes. In a large national survey of professionals and others concerned with under-eights (across all sectors – education, social services and voluntary provision) 'knowledge of child development' was considered the prime requirement by both heads and practioners (Blenkin and Yue, 1994). Those surveyed also believed that everyone working with young children, in whatever capacity, should have the experience of carrying out a child study that involved planned observation.

During the 1990s the number of day-care places offered by the independent sector has increased dramatically, while opportunities for training and the study of child development have declined. Certainly the new National Vocational Qualifications and registration systems ensure that basic standards are maintained. What is not being fostered, on the other hand, is adults' perceptive understanding of children.

Finally, the Children Act (1989) has important implications for all practitioners working with young children and families. The Act claims to put the child first: the needs and wishes of the child are to be paramount. If this aspiration is to be achieved, however, adults working with children need to be particularly well-informed, conscious not merely of children's general development and the appropriate means of studying and communicating with them, but also understanding their individuality within particular cultural contexts.

Britain is a far less child-centred country than most of its neighbours. One recent publication, *Children First* (Leach, 1994), makes a well-argued case for all adults to be much more aware of children and much more sensitive towards them; to recognise the need to 'get alongside children'. The old saying has it that 'children should be seen and not heard'. In Britain today it sometimes seems that children are not even 'seen'.

References

Baldwin, M. (1994) 'Why observe children?' *Social Work Education 13*, 2, 74–85.

Blenkin, G. and Yue, N. (1994) 'Profiling early years practitioners: Some first impressions from a national survey.' *Early Years 15*, 1, 13–22.

CCETSW (1991) *The Teaching of Child Care in the Diploma in Social Work.* London: CCETSW.

Leach, P. (1994) *Children First.* London: Michael Joseph.

McMahon, L. and Farnfield, S. (1994) 'Infant and child observation as preparation for social work practice.' *Social Work Education 13*, 3, 81–98.

Miller, L., Rustin, M., Rustin, M. and Shuttleworth, J. (1989) *Closely Observed Infants.* London: Duckworth.

Noyes, P. for the Department of Health (1991) *Child Abuse: A Study of Inquiry Reports.* London: HMSO.

Phillips, M. for the Department of Health (1988) *Protecting Children: A Guide for Social Workers undertaking a Comprehensive Assessment.* London: HMSO.

Trowell, J. and Miles, G. (1991) 'The contribution of observation to professional development in social work.' *Journal of Social Work Practice 5*, 1.

Wilson, K. (1992) 'The place of observation in social work training.' *Journal of Social Work Practice 6*, 1, 37–47.

CHAPTER TWO

Changing Views of Child Observation

Historical perspectives

Observation has a long history. Thoughtful observers of animal and human life have given us great art, from the pre-historic cave painters to artists of our own age. Scientists too have long been careful observers of the world around them and have developed and improved ways of seeing it. They have extended the limits of the human eye with ingenious devices such as microscopes, telescopes, X-rays, sensors and ultra-sonic scanners. Cameras and video recorders have added another dimension. We can now see events over and over again.

The recording of children's behaviour is also not a new idea, but has a notable tradition. The simplest form of observation record is the diary entry. Parents, and others, from very different backgrounds have noted children's progress and activities for centuries. All that was necessary was writing ability and motivation. Typically the first smile, the appearance of teeth, when the child first walked, or accounts of illnesses were all documented.

Such very personal, anecdotal records may be fascinating and offer insights into a family's private life, but they cannot provide reliable, truly objective information. Often the observed behaviour is intermingled with personal interpretations of the child's actions. The subject has not been randomly selected from the general population, nor picked out as a representative of a particular group. The infant or child is being observed simply as a precious individual, a special member of the family.

From at least the seventeenth century books have been appearing that offer guidance on how to bring children up properly and how to train and educate them. A change in attitude is detectable from the later eighteenth century under the influence of Jean-Jacques Rousseau's writings. Rousseau believed that children's natural development should be recognised and fostered, and that the didactic practices of adults at that time might be harmful. In his view the behaviour of the child was a legitimate area of study in its own right. One of the first significant publications after Rousseau's ground-breaking book *Émile, or On Education* (1762) was the work of a Swiss theorist, Johann Heinrich Pestalozzi (1746–1827), who in 1774 published a record of his son's early development. A decade or so later, in Germany, Dietrich Tiedemann similarly produced a written account of *his* son's first three years. What should be recognised here is that these were books of a new kind, and led to a realisation in the nineteenth century that the child is a thinking person worthy of study and investigation and that natural behaviour is a valuable aid to understanding the child's mind. From now on presumptions about the nature of children, and how they should be educated, trained and disciplined, would increasingly be challenged.

Perhaps the greatest stimulus to systematic child study was the work of Charles Darwin (1809–1882). It is hard for us now to appreciate the tremendous impact of the publication *On The Origin of Species* (1859). 'If a new sun had appeared in the sky, the astonishment of educated men from San Francisco to Moscow, from Melbourne to Bergen, could hardly have been greater than it was then' (Wilhelm quoted in Kessen, 1965, p.131). While writing this seminal work, Darwin was closely observing his children, especially his first-born, 'Doddy' (William Erasmus Darwin). His acute observations – '... saw him smile, not only with his lips but eyes...' (see Kessen, 1965) – reveal a very sensitive observer as well as an affectionate father. The motives for the record-keeping went beyond those of an interested, loving parent. He was deliberately looking for parallels between primitive man and the child – indeed he believed that in a developing child he was seeing the process of evolution itself. His subsequent studies comparing humans with other species, presented in *The Expression of Emotions in Man and Animals* (1872) drew directly on these observations of children, though the actual records of Doddy's early life were not finally published until 1887, some 37 years after he had made them. He was prompted to make public his observations of his son's first three years after reading H. Taine's account of the mental development of an infant (in the journal *Mind*). Darwin's reponse to this description was to publish an article 'Biographical Sketch of an Infant' in the journal *Mind* (1887):

> During the first seven days various reflex actions, namely sneezing, hiccoughing, yawning, stretching, and of course sucking and screaming, were well performed by my infant. On the seventh day, I touched the naked sole of his foot with a bit of paper, and he jerked it away, curling at the same time his toes, like a much older child when tickled. The perfection of these reflex movements shows that the extreme imperfection of the voluntary ones is not due to the state of the muscles or of the coordinating centres. At this time, though so early, it seemed clear to me that a warm soft hand applied to his face excited a wish to suck. This must be considered as a reflex or an instinctive action, for it is impossible to believe that the experience and association with the touch of his mother's breast could so soon have come into play. During the first fortnight he often started on hearing any sudden sound, and blinked his eyes. The same fact was observed in some of my other infants within the first fortnight. Once, when he was sixty-six days old, I happened to sneeze, and he started violently, frowned, looked frightened, and cried rather badly: for an hour afterwards he was in a state which would be called nervous in an older person, for every slight sound made him start. (Darwin, quoted in Kessen, 1965, pp.118–119)

In the same article he hypothesises about gender-specific behaviour in the same child who, at two years three months, had been throwing books and sticks at '... anyone who offended him; and so it was with some of my other sons. On the other hand, I could never see a trace of such aptitude in my infant daughters; and this makes me think that a tendency to throw objects is inherited by boys.' He also makes comparisons with animals, contrasting the expression of jealousy in children and dogs.

Darwin's fame brought the 'baby biography' to public attention. Here was an important method for the study of children which was academically respectable.

However, the child study published by Wilhelm Preyer and based on the first three years of *his* son's life is generally agreed to be the first proper child study, even if not wholly accurate. For example, Preyer, a physiologist, mistakenly asserted:

> First days, all children deaf. Fourth day, child hears noises like clapping of hands. Eleventh and twelfth days, child quieted by father's voice: hears whistling. (1889, p.x)

But his fine observation of another child, unusually a girl, is worth quoting:

> A litle girl in the eleventh month found her chief pleasure in 'rummaging' with trifles in drawers and in little boxes... the eagerness and seriousness with which such apparently aimless movements are performed, is remarkable... This is not mere playing, although it is so-called; it is *experimenting* (his italics). (In Kessen, 1965, p.143)

The next significant figure was the American psychologist Granville Stanley Hall (1846–1924). His child study, *The Content of Children's Minds* (1883), went beyond observation, since he chose to question the children themselves. Child questionnaires henceforth became a fashionable new tool for information-gathering. Hall's work was a powerful impetus for the development of child psychology especially in the USA. He had a deep interest in children 'as they really are'. Some of the quality of this commitment is revealed in a paper with the title 'The Story of a Sand Pile', which documents his observations of a group of children when presented with a large load of sand. His interest in this episode focuses particularly on the children's creative and vigorous response to this interesting opportunity, in '... digging, exploring, constructing, destroying...'. Among his many initiatives, Hall introduced the writings of Wilhelm Preyer to the American public, encouraging mothers to follow Preyer's example and keep records of their own infant's development. He also brought Sigmund Freud over from Europe on a lecture tour.

By 1900 child study had become an essential tool in the investigation of human development, used by professionals and the general public alike. The drive to make it even more scientific led to the establishment of special child study centres at universities across the USA. Parents were requested to bring their children to laboratory nursery schools so that observations could be conducted in controlled surroundings. Psychologists and educationalists were becoming deeply interested in the early years of childhood and their potential significance. They wanted to discover the 'normal' sequence of development. A specialised journal *Child Study Monthly* was launched in the 1890s.

Nonetheless, critics of the laboratory-based controlled experiments with small children began to voice their scepticism and to publish alternative studies. Anthropologists, most famously Margaret Mead, went out into the natural environment collecting evidence for their case studies (or field studies as they called them). Their criticism of the laboratory studies seems obvious to us now, for the behaviour of young children must be affected, even distorted, by placing them in an unusual environment. Barker and Wright, two American 'ecological psychologists', appreciated not only that behaviour outside the laboratory would be quite different but also that experimental research on children typically carried out by psychologists bore little relation to what children were familiar with in their daily lives. By contrast, Barker and Wright's classic study, *One Boy's Day* (1951), is precisely what it suggests. They had attempted to document, without any interference, the natural stream of behaviour of one seven-year-old boy from the moment he got up to when he went to bed. The authors argued that, though it can be very difficult for observers to avoid altering the phenomenon they are investigating, children are particularly unselfconscious and will probably not display uncharacteristic patterns of behaviour for any length of time. The snag with naturalistic observation is the problem of organising the enormous quantity of data generated. Its great strength, though, is that it does portray the full range and complexity of behaviour. The *ecological* approach we have just been considering alerts us to the need to take account of the child's real habitat: the location, other people present, and the expectations and rules under which the child is operating.

Back in Europe observations were also being made which have had long-term consequences on the way children are viewed. Sigmund Freud (1856–1939) proposed various highly influential theories, based on his own observations, about the development of personality and the significance of early experiences. Valid or otherwise, these have become part of everyday 'knowledge'. In Switzerland Jean Piaget (1886–1980) kept records of his three children's behaviour from when they were newly born. He himself was almost a child prodigy, publishing his first academic article on bird behaviour in a learned journal by the age of fourteen. He had his degree by eighteen and doctorate by twenty-one. Though originally a biologist and zoologist, he became intrigued by the way young human beings seem to construct their own understanding of the world. The study of epistemology (the development of knowledge and understanding) absorbed him throughout his long and productive life (Chapter Five will outline his theoretical perspectives).

In Britain the work of Susan Isaacs (1885–1948) has had a noticeable impact on thinking about young children and how they learn through their own explorations. Her world-famous Malting House Nursery (in Cambridge) gave children basic resources with which to play, to create and investigate, under minimum 'adult interference'. Isaacs' classic books, *Intellectual Growth in Young Children* (1930) and *Social Development in Young Children* (1933) are based entirely on her observations. They show children, in her words, 'as living individuals'.

Two other famous observers need to be mentioned for their rather different techniques and perspectives. Konrad Lorenz and Niko Tinbergen were both zoologists and their method is known as *ethology*. The ethologist sets out to catalogue behaviour such as body movements and facial expressions, and to correlate observations with the stimuli which cause them. While this method has occasionally been adapted to the study of children (e.g. Blurton-Jones, 1972), it has been more generally used by animal scientists. Lorenz and Tinbergen, for example, have respectively investigated geese and herring gulls in this way.

Because there is potential confusion between the concepts of ecological and ethological studies, it may be helpful to clarify them. In terms of similarity, both are concerned with observing unobtrusively, in a way that manipulates neither the environment nor the subjects. They both attempt to describe behaviour in natural settings. Where they differ is in terms of breadth. Ecologists generally focus on fairly *large* units of behaviour – for example, sand play. On the other hand ethologists focus on *smaller* units – facial expressions, gestures, body posture and eye gaze. Ecologists are more interested in the purpose and sense of the episode, while ethologists concentrate on behaviour patterns. Ecologists are advised to describe the quality of actions (e.g. *how* things are done) whereas the ethologist would regard qualitative phrases as unscientific.

Contemporary views of child development

The march of history can be presented to seem like a positive, cumulative progression towards a superior present-day pinnacle of understanding. With regard to everyday, taken-for-granted general 'knowledge' about children at the end of the twentieth century, it is true that there is extensive factual information available even though there are still enormous gaps as well as many conflicting opinions. One must always be ready to question the validity of knowledge. It may prove to be less coherent and objective, less securely based, than it seems at first. In the last section we traced the history of the observational study of children. We saw that some of these studies led to the construction of theories about development. In evaluating these and any other theories it is critically important to investigate the circumstances which led to the generation of the theory in the first place. When was the research carried out? What was the nature and size of the sample on which the theory was based? What kinds of hypotheses were already in the mind of the researcher? And what kind of 'mind-set' did he (usually he) have as he set about interpreting the data? These are some of the questions to be asked. In this section four important theoretical perspectives on child development will be examined: developmental 'norms', attachment, cognitive development, and a cultural and ecological view of development.

Developmental 'norms'

Developmental 'norms' are the sequential steps through which all children can be expected to progress. Typically these are considered under headings such as physical, cognitive, social and emotional development (though some would add other categories – for instance, communication and moral development). Within each category the stages of development are usually presented in hierarchical form starting with the simplest. The stages are usually linked to children's ages. We might well ask where these norms have come from. Their primary source is the work of American psychologists, especially Arnold Gesell, during the first half of the twentieth century. Through observations of children, often in laboratory settings, and through the collection of data, they created a structure which has formed the basis for the assessment of children ever since. Developmental norms are referred to not only by professionals. Parents too draw on them to judge their children's progress. The same norms are also used the world over; they are not restricted to their country of origin.

It is disconcerting to ponder the sources of this profoundly influential work. The researchers were almost without exception male, white, middle-class psychologists. Their research aim was to identify the universal, normal stages of development through which *all* children pass. Their subjects, though, were virtually all white and living in the relatively prosperous United States of the twentieth century. Information was gathered in the special child study centres attached to universities (and indeed information continues to be gathered in the 'clinical' setting of university laboratories). Ben Bradley's (1989) criticisms bring the issue sharply into focus:

> Much experimental work on infancy takes place *in vitro* – on the social equivalent of a desert island... there is no way for most studies to represent the different anxieties, responsibilities, standards of living, demands of other children, interpersonal relationships and work commitments which shape the lives of parents, and hence of their children. Many studies focus only on well-educated, middle-class mothers with small families. (p.155)

The same critic also reminds us how far these settings are from the reality of life for many. It is after all estimated that at least forty per cent of the world's population live in poverty. Disease and starvation are rife. 'Domestic violence continues, marriages break up, wars rage on, prescriptions for tranquillisers and stress-related diseases run at record levels.' (*ibid* p.157)

Mary Sheridan's *Children's Developmental Progress* (1973) is an example of the way an influential handbook can shape thinking for decades. As a medical doctor, Sheridan selected for her framework what she termed 'the four outstanding human *biological* [my italics] achievements' – Posture and Large Movements, Vision and Fine Movements, Hearing and Speech, and Social Behaviour and Play. Readers will note that there is no separate category for cognitive development. She developed her 'Stycar sequences' from observations and photographs of the children with whom she came into contact during the 1950s. Her book, first published in 1960, is still being regularly reprinted and still forms the basis of official guidelines for social workers from the Department of Health (Phillips, 1988). The general acceptance and very widespread use of the Sheridan guidelines for all children, no matter how extraordinarily different their situation, is at last being challenged. Comparative studies of the very different cultural styles of caring for young children worldwide have sharpened awareness of the variety and flexibility of human development. Scepticism has also arisen about the dangerous effects of prescriptive guidelines or checklists on parents. The checklist mentality can result in parental anxieties, competitive attitudes, over- or under-expectation, and rigidity of thinking about children's progress. More recently the many subtle effects of gender difference in child development have also become clearer. Furthermore, the assessment of children with disabilities all too often relies on the use of scales of 'normal' development, making it difficult to strike a balance between identifying where help is needed while still valuing the positive, unproblematic aspects of the child's development. The unique individuality of every growing person can easily be devalued by over-concentration on measurement and the achievement of norms.

On the other hand, some kind of guide to the milestones or steps of general development is valuable. Jennie Lindon's recent handbook (1993) presents a balanced account which at the same time recognises the multi-cultural nature of the UK. Until comparatively recently very few texts on child development have considered the implications of an anti-racist perspective. The Working Group Against Racism in Children's Resources (WGARCR), however, has had a working group on the topic for some years. Their *Guidelines for the Selection and Evaluation of Child Development Books* (1991) helps the reader to recognise the values and assumptions that underlie and reinforce racism; to be conscious of the transmission of blatant or subtle racist messages; to value diversity of child-rearing practices and to question the usefulness of certain texts on child development. They actually found that very few were written from an anti-racist, multi-cultural and multi-lingual perspective. Nor did the literature usually acknowledge any form of discrimination in terms of social class, disability and gender difference or orientation. The topic of child development will be discussed further in Chapter Five.

Attachment

The way that adults perceive children and the experiences children receive through their parents are likely to be influenced by their concept of 'attachment'. One definition of 'attachment' is the close, continuous relationship with one other person that human beings need in order to develop a confident, stable, integrated personality. Attachment theory is predominantly associated with the name of John Bowlby (1907–1980), a British psychiatrist. The circumstances leading to the creation of the theory are a telling example of the significance of knowing the context. After World War II, Bowlby was commissioned by the World Health Organisation to investigate the plight of children who were orphaned or separated from their parents as a consequence of the devastating conflict in Europe. These children were all in some kind of care – with foster parents or in institutions. Out of his research and reflections he concluded that without an intense, close relationship with a mother in the first three years a child was doomed, since '...mother love in infancy and childhood is as important for mental health as are vitamins and protein for physical health' (1951). He later (1969) went so far as to say that any psychiatric disorder can be linked to an impaired capacity for bonding and that such disorders in later life are frequently the result of some disturbance in bonding in early childhood. He believed that certain conditions were absolutely essential. The child must have a loving relationship with one particular person (usually the mother), that the resulting attachment must continue unbroken for the first three years, that it should ideally be centred within the child's own family and offer adequate stimulation. In the 1990s it is hard to grasp the powerful impact of Bowlby's publications some forty years ago. Politicians found his thesis useful in validating their decisions to close day nurseries and encourage women back into the home. There were strong social pressures persuading women to care for their children twenty-four hours a day (even if this was not exactly what Bowlby had said) and to do otherwise would be damaging. Bowlby's studies left out consideration of the more communal shared care of children which is commonplace in many cultural groups outside Europe. We now recognise that such shared child rearing is very much more beneficial for the mental health of women than the rather closed, private style common in the UK where parent and child are in a 'monotropic' relationship (comparable to monogamy). Michael Rutter's important critique, *Maternal Deprivation Reassessed* (1972), and other research reports have restored the balance. If anything, the danger now is that attachment, and all that it entails, is not given the emphasis it deserves. Chapter Five includes two sections which explore attachment in relation to observations.

Cognitive development

Jean Piaget has already been introduced, and his background in biology and zoology noted. Because of his biological framework he underlined the processes by which innate tendencies motivate the developing person to interact with the environment. Piaget was yet another white, male European whose theories have been revered the world over. His 'stage' theory of cognitive development was generated through his observations and through setting children special tasks and questioning them on what they were doing. His so-called 'clinical interviewing' has, over the years, been replicated in many countries. The special tasks are said to give insight into the different styles of thinking at successive stages of development.

To give a famous example, children under six will claim, when asked, that there is more liquid in a tall thin glass than a short, squat one, even though they have seen the very same liquid poured from one glass to the other. (See Chapter Five of this book on the development of thinking.)

Piaget's work has been subjected to much scrutiny. Among the key criticisms of his ideas several stand out. First, he gave insufficient emphasis to language and social aspects. Second, his concept of egocentricity (which seems to have captured popular imagination) leads to a devaluing of small children. Third, Piagetian stage theory has had the unfortunate negative effect of restricting the thinking of some educators of young children. Fourth, Piaget implied that children lack logic, disregarding the fact that, in being asked to make sense of logical problems, children are affected by the nature of the task they are set, and in particular try to 'read' what the adults expect of them. Finally he failed to recognise the significance of the cultural context. Indeed Piaget believed that the development of the mind was independent of its social environment. Some have portrayed the Piagetian child as a 'lonely scientist' trying to make sense of the world by her/his own efforts.

A cultural and ecological view of development

Drawing on an entirely different view of development, Lev Vygotsky (1896–1934), and his colleagues in Russia challenged the Piagetian view that the formation of the basic structures in the human mind is universally the same and not dependent on the child's cultural environment. In contrast to the perception of the child as a 'lonely scientist', Vygotsky saw the child's development as deeply embedded in a society, the child being a meaningful member of a cultural group from birth. Vygotsky's theory evolved in its own historical and geographical context. During the 1920s and 1930s (in Leninist and Stalinist times) Vygotsky travelled across the USSR observing the diverse cultural patterns in which young children were being brought up – from nomadic to relatively sophisticated urban communities, from the Siberian cold to the comparatively lush Georgian farmlands.

Vygotsky's scattered writings are only just becoming integrated into our thinking in the west, and the insights derived from his thinking have still to make their full impact. Nevertheless the deep significance of the cultural group in Vygotskian theory is clear:

> ... in the process of development, children begin to use the same forms of behaviour in relation to themselves that others used in relation to them. Children master the social forms of behaviour and transfer these forms to themselves... Any function in the child's cultural development appears twice, or on two planes. First it appears on the social plane, and then on the psychological plane. (Vygotsky, quoted in Meadows, 1993, p.237)

The development of language and of adults' support of children's learning are major issues in Vygotsky's work and will be discussed later (Chapter Five). Barbara Rogoff (1990), in her development of Vygotsky's work, emphasises that while all humans share a great deal of universal activity (learning to walk, speaking a language, etc.) there is nevertheless great variety in styles of living. In particular, each community will have its own goals for children's development, what she calls 'valued skills'.

One other psychologist, Urie Bronfenbrenner, must be included in this chapter. His *Ecology of Human Development* (1979) similarly draws on cross-cultural comparisons of families bringing up children. His ecological perspective widens the context for development still further to include not only the child's immediate family and cultural group but the total setting in which that community finds itself. This brings in such matters as the legal framework, economic and employment possibilities, and finally the wider beliefs, ideologies and attitudes current at that time. Bronfenbrenner gave labels to these settings or systems and compared them to the nesting arrangements of Russian dolls, one within another. The child (the smallest doll, as it were) belongs to one or more *micro-systems* (the family, the school etc.). The interactions between the various micro-systems he called *meso-systems* (for example the relationships between family and school, family and neighbourhood). Beyond the meso-systems are the *exo-systems*, to which children do not normally have access (these include local government and the parents' workplaces). The largest outer 'Russian doll', the *macro-system*, refers to the ideological contexts – attitudes, values and beliefs generally held by the population at large (especially reflected in the media).

The observer's views of children and development

When we observe we are liable to think that we are seeing what anyone else would see. This is an illusion, for what we 'see' depends on what we bring to the observation in our own minds. We bring values and beliefs about ourselves, other people and the world, which we may rarely talk about or even consciously consider. But students learning about children and observation (for whatever professional field) have a responsibility to think carefully about their own attitudes, for these are bound to affect and limit observation. Further, this personal development of self-awareness is also necessary in preparing for anti-oppressive practice in future professional work. First then, we must recognise that we all have different definitions of ourselves, and that this personal definition includes our own ethnic or national origin, age, class, religion, physical appearance, gender and sexual orientation. Second, we need to consider where we are in relation to others: where we stand in society, the personal power we have, and how we perceive others from different groups. Finally, we must inform ourselves about structural oppressions in society.

Reflection on the source of personal understandings and beliefs is a productive first step. We can start by looking at our own childhood. The rules, roles and 'indoctrination' we have experienced as children almost certainly linger on (though we may react strongly against them): notions about smacking and punishment of children, attitudes towards food, ideas about appropriate dress, bias against other social groups, suspicions and intolerance of mental illness. (For some activities on this topic see Drummond et al., 1992.) Outside the family, our schooling will further have been responsible for forming opinions. Did we share the playground with children of all social classes? Were we at a single-sex school? Was the local dialect regarded as inferior, to be eradicated?

Looking back on these early experiences it is well to remember, as J.P. Hartley said in The Go-Between, 'The past is a foreign country.' For many people the changes in the last forty years have been the greatest ever known in a lifetime. Women's roles, family structures, life-styles have been transformed. The availability of personal transport, television and video have altered many peoples' life experiences and consequently their perceptions. We need to be very aware of the continuing power and influence of the media, especially television, in shaping our views, including the portrayal of children and childhood in a way which denies reality.

The notion of childhood as a time of innocence and ignorance is too often assumed and accepted by the general public. In fact children as young as three are quite clear about gender and racial difference, and they will have almost certainly have seen sexual intercourse and violence on the television screen. By five years old they know the values society ascribes to women and girls as well as to different skin colours (Milner, 1983;

Siraj-Blatchford, 1994). Other information about children and their development and 'needs' is also likely to be filtered through fashionable media perspectives. As we have seen, even specialised literature must be treated with caution and scepticism. Until comparatively recently the way that professionals have conceptualised children and their development has been dominated by the work of psychologists and scientific approaches. The complexity and entirety of the human experience (the 'holistic' standpoint) have simply not been acknowledged. In addition, Western norms have been used indiscriminately.

The final section of this chapter aims to alert the reader to some areas of potential bias. It is not comprehensive and students will need to read more widely and, it is hoped, share these topics in discussion with others. Culture, language, physical appearance and gender are the four topics to be considered. There is clearly overlap between some of these, but looking at them separately may help to clarify understanding. (Incidently, the order given has nothing to do with hierarchy.)

Cultural perspectives

Culture is an over-used word with many shades of meaning. In this context it will be taken to mean a 'shared pattern of living'. As such it is not static, but continually evolving. It includes class and shared religious beliefs. There is a tendency to focus on the more familiar tokens of culture that we all inherit – the music and songs, myths and legends, food and clothing, home objects – but as important, though perhaps less obvious, is the 'shared total communication framework'. Within our cultural group we share not just the spoken and written words of our language, but also gestures and actions, tones of voice and facial expressions. These different aspects of communication are always present but remain invisible as long as we stay within our familiar culture. We employ them unconsciously.

When observing or communicating with members of other cultures we are more likely to notice them. In her book, *Multicultural Issues in Child Care* (1993), Janet Gonzalez-Mena urges the importance of developing sensitive observational skills if we want to be good at communicating with children and adults. She has picked out five areas in which students need to learn communication skills, even though they may share a common language. These concern smiling, eye-contact, sensitivity to personal space, touch and time concepts. The frequency of smiling is very variable across cultures. Russians tend to smile only in the context of humour, rather than use it as a friendly overture. During Cold War exchanges, the broad smile of the American greeting was taken by the Russians as evidence either that the other side lacked intelligence or that the smile was fake. On the other hand the Americans thought the Russians cold and unfriendly. In some Asian and African cultural groups eye-contact between adults would be seen as insolence, whereas to some English people a lack of eye-contact is interpreted as shiftiness. People from rural and urban districts may have very different expectations of appropriate personal space. Pease (1981, p.23) reports on the problems encountered in Australia by a Danish couple whose behaviour was considered to be overtly sexual. The problem was that Europeans typically are comfortable with a personal space of 20–30 centimetres, while for Australians the comparable figure is apparantly 46 centimetres, so the close proximity of the Danes was misinterpreted. Some rural people may have a much greater personal zone, as much as six metres, according to Pease.

In addition, each cultural group has its own shared patterns of up-bringing and likewise particular goals for its children. (Chapter Six considers different cultural perspectives on children's behaviour in pre-school.) One example is the taken-for-granted, middle-class, Western practice of placing babies to sleep alone in a separate room, which is seen as cruel in some cultures and contrasts strongly with the expectation that an infant should naturally sleep with the mother. Styles of bringing up children are not immune to change. Within a generation customs can be transformed as a result of education, the redefining of women's roles, the commercial availability of goods and conveniences, and changing work patterns.

Language

The observer's views about language use may well be influenced by attitudes in society on the status of different languages. Western languages such as French still seem to be held in higher regard than the 'home' languages of ethnic communities in the UK, for example Urdu. This is a curious fact, but the attitude to bilingualism is even more curious '… in British education and care systems being bilingual is still too often perceived as an aberration, or worse, as something children should grow out of' (Siraj-Blatchford, 1994). When one considers that over seventy per cent of the world's population uses more than one language, this narrow perspective is especially depressing. Children whose first language at home is not English are thus seen as *being* a problem and *having* a problem when the evidence is that learning two languages is beneficial to the speaker. Bilingualism actually helps the development of language (Hazareesingh *et al.*, 1989) for among other things learners become more aware of alternative forms of expression (a dog can also be called *un chien*). They become more alive to emotional expressions (e.g. they are better able to interpret facial expressions, gestures and tone of voice), they have greater social sensitivity and improved concept formation. Bilingualism should rather be seen as a strength, and valued as such. Siraj-Blatchford provides a very useful chapter on the subject (1994).

The use of dialect is commonly under-valued, and a hierarchy can be discerned here. The accents of rural Aberdeenshire or Devon tend to be preferred to the urban accents of Glasgow and Birmingham. There are notions too about what constitutes 'good' and 'bad' English – notions which are subtly changing all the time, for language is not static, it evolves. In connection with the observation of small children expectations about linguistic progress may colour perceptions. Apparent mispronounciations (sometimes romanticised and regarded as 'cute') are often very common. Two instances of this typical developmental stage are '*wabbit*' for rabbit and '*fis*' for fish. Children often over-apply certain grammatical forms, such as the -ed ending of the past tense, 'I went to the shops and *buyed* some biscuits.' This is actually an indication that the child understands the principle of forming the past tense rather than a mistake. Language will be one of the themes for study in Chapter Five.

Physical appearance

Beauty may be superficial, but the 'image', the outer appearance, influences our impression of a person. Healthy, properly nourished, well-groomed, alert young children are very appealing. For survival the human infant must be 'attractive' to the caring adults, so the 'baby' features of chubby face, big wide eyes, and soft skin are part of nature's way of ensuring the interest of the adults. Some adults are especially charmed by the beauty and seeming innocence of children. The young of all ethnic groups can have this quality; it is not restricted to Barbie-doll look-alikes.

On the other hand, some children do not have an aura of loveliness. They may seem dull and lifeless, awkward, unkempt, thin and miserable. There are two more aspects of children's appearance which can influence the observer. These are size and apparent maturity. Some children look much older or younger than they really are. All these factors can very forcefully affect adults' perceptions and expectations of children. We may be at risk of condoning unacceptable behaviour, or not believing that a child is capable of doing something unkind, because they look so beautifully innocent. The opposite may well result too, so that the lack-lustre child is not credited with achievements. It is well-known that children who appear older than their true age can be at a serious disadvantage when behaviour does not meet expectations.

Observers and workers with young children may well find themselves drawn to some children rather than others (though they will of course try to maintain an even-handed, professional stance). If a child has to be selected for observation it is therefore best to find some way of random-ising the choice. Perhaps choosing the first child who comes in wearing something blue, or taking a letter from the alphabet and finding the first name on the list starting with that letter.

'Race' is a word which needs defining, even though scientists accept that it has no real genetic basis, that it is in fact literally 'skin deep'. It refers purely to physiological difference – skin colour, hair type and some facial features. But while in some ways it is so superficial, it has long been used, and still is, to group people and to grant them greater or lesser status accordingly. As Iram Siraj-Blatchford (1994) puts it:

> White scientists invented racial categories and, given the history of white domination and exploitation of black people, they put themselves at the top of their racial hierarchy... most British people still believe or act according to this racist structure. (p.4)

Much racism is still unrecognised, covert and insidious, and because it is fundamentally to do with power (prejudice in combination with power creates racism) it is particularly dangerous and difficult to counter and eradicate.

Gambe et al. (1992), in a training manual for social workers, draw attention to three areas of risk – exclusion (that is ignoring the existence of 'race', claiming to be 'colour-blind' and stating that 'I treat them all the same'); tokenism (in other words, paying attention to 'race' only as an afterthought); and pathology (seeing other groups as strange, different and inferior). This last area is most significant in observation. In a recent article (1994) Owusu-Bempah investigated the hypothesis that 'Many people seem to accept, as self-evident, the notion that black children harbour unfavourable cognitions about themselves and their racial group, and that they would rather be white'. He found the myth still to be widespread among social work students. Interpretations of children's behaviour and needs are still based on the dangerous notion of widespread negative self-concepts – suggesting that black children's friendships with white are therefore 'pathological'. By viewing children in this way there is a strong risk of self-fulfilling effects and a compounding of latent difficulties. Concepts of self and attitudes within communities are not static. Many young black British people have positive self-images, especially in the more multi-cultural areas of Britain. However, somewhat isolated members of minority groups may have more negative feelings about themselves. Observation studies should give students the opportunity to consider these issues and observe as objectively as possible, listening very carefully to what children and adults are really saying.

Gender

Pre-school settings, where some children will spend the greater part of their day, are not small oases apart from the 'real' world. Attitudes and behaviour with regard to women and men in the outside world do impinge. Indeed at the pre-school stage gender imbalances and inequalities are especially evident.

The responsibilities for the care of the youngest children are traditionally seen as belonging to women; not only do these responsibilities rest on women in the individual family, but also more generally in society. The care and education of pre-school children is seen as women's work. It may well be the case that women are much better suited to the very diverse, responsive types of skill which are demanded. Women are usually more comfortable with a nurturing and holistic approach, and staff in pre-school groups inescapably find themselves switching rapidly between very basic physical caring and challenging intellectual response and stimulation. Many men, however, feel ill at ease in the practical caring of young children. They prefer to concentrate on single defined tasks, rather than constantly switching their attention. But there are other reasons too for the lack of males in pre-school employment. It is perceived as lowly, poorly paid and lacking in promotion prospects, and primarily as 'women's work'. Women are likely to have similar views. It is increasingly clear that the status of work with this age group must be improved and women's special characteristics, skills and achievements better valued. If this could be achieved, the self-esteem and confidence of women working with young children should grow markedly. Jillian Rodd (1994) has studied the concept of leadership in the early years and writes of the importance of raising the professionalism of these women. The question of status is part of a wider problem which affects hierarchies of employment generally. Even though more and more women are in employment (much of it part-time, because they wish to maintain their caring roles at home), they are very rarely in top, decision-making posts (Social Focus on Women,1995). So patriarchal, male power is still dominant.

Yet there is more to the gender issue in pre-schools than the serious absence of men (with the message that this gives) and the consequent lack of male role models for children at a developmentally crucial stage (see Chapter Five, *Gender Differences in Pre-school*). The very nature of the resources chosen, the activities, and the attitudes of the staff may all influence children's perceptions of gender roles. Pre-schools have a tendency to be conservative, traditional places. Stereotypes tend not to be challenged and staff may not realise how their choices of equipment or their responses to children can have long-term consequences. Student observers, on the other hand, may notice, as researchers like Julia Hodgeon have, that female staff are more likely to join in play in the home corner or with table-top toys such as jigsaw puzzles but will avoid taking part in 'messier' activities or mechanical construction (reported in Skelton,1991).

The allocation of tasks by requests such as: 'Which big, strong boys are going to help me shift the computer?' or 'I need some girls to tidy up the home corner' are not at all uncommon. Staff perceptions of boys and girls are widely different. Boys are seen as dynamic but posing more problems, whereas girls are viewed more favourably as being easier to manage. (Several research examples are given in Skelton, 1991, and Croll and Moses, 1991.) Moreover, staff reactions are likely to reinforce the girls' reticence and the boys' confidence. (See Chapter Five for more on staff attention to boys and girls.)

As suggested above, the selection of resources for children will also shape their play experiences and reinforce social conditioning. 'Action man' and 'Barbie doll' (selling many millions around the world every year) symbolise the potential of stereotyping toys. In *Playing them False* (1989) Dixon reveals how seemingly innocuous play equipment is part of 'big business' and a force to be reckoned with. In addition books, posters and the content of a considerable number of traditional stories are all possible sources of stereotyped gender roles. From a somewhat different angle it is thought that the more spatial activities that boys engage in enhance their scientific and mathematical understanding, while the emphasis on social interaction of girls' play improves their language, and in turn their literacy skills.

We still need to know much more about the effects of pre-school experiences on later development and gender awareness. Research is especially necessary to explore the links between gender and *race*, in the light of evidence that seven-year-old black girls are higher achievers than black boys, white boys and indeed white girls (Tizard *et al.*, 1988).

Professional bias

While many readers of this book will just be starting out on a professional career, others may have been working with children and families for some years. In the course of professional preparation one is bound to absorb the priorities, ethos, methods and styles of problem-solving of that profession, as well as a particular way of viewing the people one is responsible for. Training, as it should, does make a difference. An inter-professional group engaged in-service training will find a rich vein for discussion as they compare their sometimes divergent interpretations of observation. In one actual case, a mixed group of nursery teachers and nursery nurses was shown an illustration of a young child standing on a high stool wielding a pair of scissors while 'cutting' some foliage (an illustration in Drummond *et al.*, 1992). Analysing their reactions to the illustration, they were sharply divided according to their training back-grounds. The teachers concentrated approvingly on the pleasure and interest the child displayed in the imaginative activity, while the nursery nurses felt the child was not being adequately safeguarded by the adults and was at risk of falling and being hurt by the scissors. Social workers, health staff, psychologists, teachers and so on will all have different perspectives and interests. This topic will be considered further in Chapter Six which looks at Assessment.

References and further reading

Barker, R.G. and Wright, H.F. (1951) *One Boy's Day: A Specimen Record of Behavior.* New York: Harper.

Blurton-Jones, N. (ed) (1972) *Ethological Studies of Child Behaviour.* Cambridge: Cambridge University Press.

Bowlby, J. (1951) *Maternal Care and Mental Health.* Geneva: World Health Organisation.

Bowlby, J. (1969) *Attachment and Loss: Vol.1. Attachment.* London: Hogarth Press.

Bradley, B.S. (1989) *Visions of Infancy.* Oxford: Basil Blackwell.

Bronfenbrenner, U. (1979) *The Ecology of Human Development.* Cambridge, MA: Harvard University Press.

Central Statistical Office (1995) *Social Focus on Women.* London: HMSO.

Croll, P. and Moses, D. (1991) 'Sex roles in the classroom.' In M. Woodhead, P. Light and R. Carr. *Growing up in a Changing Society* (Vol. 3 of the Open University series Child Development in a Social Context) London: Routledge.

Darwin, C. (1859) *On The Origin of Species.* London: John Murray.

Darwin, C. (1872) *The Expression of Emotions in Man and Animals.* London: John Murray.

Darwin, C. (1877) 'A biographical sketch of an infant.' *Mind 7,* 285–294 reprinted in W. Kessen (1965) *The Child: Perspectives in Psychology.* New York: John Wiley.

Dixon, B. (1989) *Playing Them False: A Study of Children's Toys, Games and Puzzles.* Stoke-on-Trent: Trentham Books.

Donaldson, M. (1978) *Children's Minds.* Harmondsworth: Penguin.

Drummond, M.J., Rouse, D. and Pugh, G. (1992) *Making Assessment Work: Values and Principles in Assessing Young Children's Learning.* London: NES Arnold in association with National Children's Bureau.

Gambe, D., Gomes, J., Kapur, V., Rongel, M. and Stubbs, P. (1992) *Improving Practice with Children and Families: A Training Manual.* London: Northern Curriculum Development Project (CCETSW, Leeds).

Gonzalez-Mena, J. (1993) *Multicultural Issues in Child Care.* Mountain View, Calif.: Mayfield Publishing Company.

Hazareesingh, S., Simms, K. and Anderson, P. (1989) *Educating the Whole Child: A Holistic Approach to Education in the Early Years.* London: Building Blocks (Save the Children).

Isaacs, S. (1930) *Intellectual Growth of Young Children.* London: Routledge, Kegan Paul.

Isaacs, S. (1933) *Social Development in Young Children.* London: Routledge, Kegan Paul.

Kessen, W. (1965) *The Child: Perspectives in Psychology.* New York: John Wiley.

Lindon, J. (1993) *Child Development from Birth to Eight.* London: National Children's Bureau.

Meadows, S. (1993) *The Child as Thinker.* London: Routledge.

Milner, D. (1983) *Children and Race.* London: Ward Lock Educational.

Owusu-Bempah, J. (1994) 'Race, self-identity and social work.' *British Journal of Social Work 24,* 123–136.

Pease, A. (1981) *Body Language: How to Read Other's Thoughts by their Gestures.* London: Sheldon Press.

Phillips, M. for the Department of Health (1988) *Protecting Children: A Guide for Social Workers Undertaking a Comprehensive Assessment.* London: HMSO.

Preyer, W. Translation by Brown, H.W. (1889) *The Mind of the Child, Part 11: The Development of the Intellect.* New York: D. Appleton and Co.

Rodd, J. (1994) *Leadership in Early Childhood.* Buckingham: Open University Press.

Rogoff, B. (1990) *Apprenticeship in Thinking: Cognitive Development in a Social Context.* New York: Oxford University Press.

Rousseau, J-J. (1762) *Émile, or On Education. An English translation.* New York: Basic Books (1975).

Rutter, M. (1972) *Maternal Deprivation Re-Assessed.* Harmondsworth: Penguin.

Sheridan, M. (1973) *Children's Developmental Progress from Birth to Five: The Stycar Sequences.* London: NFER. (First published 1960, several later editions.)

Siraj-Blatchford, I. (1994) *The Early Years: Laying the Foundations for Racial Equality.* Stoke-on-Trent: Trentham Books.

Skelton, C. (1991) 'Demolishing the "House that Jack Built": Anti-sexist initiatives in the primary school.' In M. Woodhead, P. Light and R. Carr. (1991) *Growing up in a Changing Society* (Vol. 3 of the Open University series, Child Development in a Social Context) London: Routledge.

Tizard, B., Blatchford, P., Burke, J., Farquhar, C. and Plewis, I. (1988) *Young Children at School in the Inner City.* Hove: Erlbaum.

Wertsch, J.V. (ed) (1985) *Culture, Communication and Cognition: Vygotskian Perspectives.* Cambridge: Cambridge University Press.

WGARCR (1991) *Guidelines for the Selection and Evaluation of Child Development Books.* London: Working Group Against Racism in Children's Resources (460 Wandsworth Road, London. SW8 3LX)

CHAPTER THREE

Pre-school Settings
The Context for Observation

Introduction

Child observation has to be actually located somewhere. Psychologists in the past attempted to make observation a clinical process by removing children from the everyday world and placing them in the 'sterile' conditions of a laboratory. It has been seen that this method creates not only practical problems but the resulting information is not necessarily more revealing, indeed behaviour may well be distorted. What must be grasped is that children are in a dynamic relationship with their environment. It is fanciful to assume that any observation can be an 'uncontaminated' record of an individual's behaviour, unaffected by the circumstances. Not only do human beings constantly respond to their changing environments, what they bring with them (personality, family, experiences, etc.) also affects those responses. Most observers will be carrying out studies in some form of pre-school setting, which in its turn will partly determine how children behave.

Significant variables in any pre-school environment include the physical circumstances (the building, its layout, the availability of outside play space, the range and quality of equipment and play materials); the ages and grouping of the children; the ratio of children to adults; and above all the quality and philosophy of the adults leading the group. In fact adults in charge of British pre-schools, once they have complied with basic legislation, have great freedom in running their group. How they accomplish this will reflect their views on the care and education of children, and the depth of their knowledge and understanding not only of children but of the children's family and cultural backgrounds.

The pre-school services you might find currently in Britain present a very fragmented, patchy picture, the diversity of provision being matched by its uneven spread. While a few services are free the majority have to be paid for by parents and in some cases the cost may be high. Furthermore there is far from adequate provision overall, in particular for the children of working parents. For over twenty years politicians of every hue have acknowledged the problem and made pledges to improve the situation, but what has been achieved in reality is still limited and unsatisfactory. This book, in addressing a primarily British readership, concentrates on our national range of provision. However, there is value in learning about practice in other countries. All our neighbours in western Europe spend relatively more than we do on this age group. Some have developed co-ordinated systems – Denmark being of particular note here. Spain too is now implementing a comprehensive plan. Other countries such Italy (mainly in the north) and Sweden offer examples of excellent practice. The final section of this chapter will briefly consider Sweden which has produced some particularly interesting research.

To return to the United Kingdom and our patchwork of pre-school services, the reason for the lack of a coherent strategy almost certainly lies in the widely held belief that very young children belong to their own family and that responsibility lies wholly with the parents. In other words the upbringing of children before school age is regarded as essentially a private matter. (Such a view is similarly widespread in the United States which also exhibits a very fragmented pre-school scene.) The role of the state is thus restricted to intervention when problems arise and legislation to regulate the services in general. Little is definite and clear, which makes it confusing for British parents and others coming fresh to the field. For a start no child is normally required to attend any kind of pre-school. Even the age at which a child may begin school itself is variable; it depends on where one lives. Children are required by law to attend school in the term following their fifth birthday (whereas the rest of the world has mostly chosen the sixth birthday as the starting age for statutory schooling). In practice a large proportion of British children start during the year in which they become five, entering the reception class when they are still four years old.

The diversity of pre-school settings for children aged one to four years may be clarified by using a simple framework of four models, each with its own rationale (These categories follow Pugh, 1989). The first model is of an *interventionist* nature. Services of this type are designed to serve only children who have been identified as being at risk or in need. Local authority funding tends to be concentrated on these children, in particular on child abuse cases. This is the one example where pre-school attendance is virtually obligatory but brings with it the risk of stigmatisation. Day nurseries and some family centres fall within this group. Second, what might be called a *universal* approach. According to this model all children in a locality, as of right, are eligible to attend a pre-school group (the aim of which is to ensure all-round development) either free or at very low cost. Local authority nursery schools are an example of this approach. The third model is based on *self-help* and *community* principles. Here a mixed set of voluntary organisations serve both adult and child needs. They are almost all self-funding and, like day care and crèche facilities, they depend on the ability of parents to meet the cost. The United Kingdom has a strong tradition of initiating and maintaining activities of this sort. Playgroups and parent/toddler groups are typical examples. The final model is primarily utilitarian. It centres on *all-day care* in order to meet the requirements of working adults. The emphasis is thus on parental needs. These services include workplace nurseries, crèches and childminding arrangements.

This chapter will set out the characteristics and basic information of eight common types of pre-school so that students become familiar with their characteristic features in advance of their visit. But before dealing with these practicalities a few more general points are worth making about the circumstances of pre-school children in to-day's Britain. Bringing up a family is profoundly affected by the economic status of parents. A third of all children are estimated to be living in poverty as the present government defines it (Kumar, 1993). Such a widespread problem directly affects pre-school provision. Lack of money and transport limits choice, while the need for many women to work creates a demand for accessible, affordable day care, which, because it is relatively low-cost, may be of second-rate quality. Furthermore, with women having to hold down a job as well as care for children and run a home, the whole family inevitably feels the pressure. A second factor having a major impact on children's lives results from changing family structures. Young children increasingly find themselves in either single-parent households (generally headed by the mother) or in 'reconstituted' families (with step-fathers and often extra 'brothers and sisters'). Since pre-schools of all kinds are also overwhelmingly run and staffed by women, concern is frequently voiced about the lack of positive male role-models for younger children. Another relevant issue is the potential for discrimination, not merely on grounds of poverty or family circumstances, but because of disability, race, language, culture or religion – all recognised as important elements by the Children Act of 1989.

The latter Act controls practically all pre-school services. It requires social services departments across the country to inspect and register all such services, both in the private and voluntary sector, wherever children are cared for during the day on a regular basis away from their parents. There are only two exceptions. First, those independent private schools which also cater for children *over* the age of five fall under the responsibility of the Department for Education. Second, local authority nursery schools and classes are also regulated by the DFE only this time through the local authority education committee. Otherwise all the fundamentals relating to pre-school services are set out in *The Children Act 1989 Guidance and Regulations Vol. 2.* (1991) – among them, regulations about space, equipment and activities, about health and safety, adult/child ratios, and the suitability of adults to work with young children.

To sum up then, the actual choice available to parents is likely to depend on where they live, their financial position, their access to transport, and the actual range of provision locally, rather than their personal preferences about what is best for their child. It may be that pragmatic forces in the end over-ride other priorities (such as quality). Vernon and Smith's (1994) finding may well be true – that parental expectations of day care services are 'neither clear nor high'.

Descriptions of the main pre-school services

Local authority day nurseries

Regulated by:	social services departments
Ages of children:	0–5 years, most commonly 18 months – 4 years
Ratio of adults to children:	1:3 (0–2 year-olds), 1:5 (3–5 year-olds)
Opening times:	full-time, e.g. 8.30a.m. – 5.30p.m all the year round.

Day nurseries have gradually narrowed their focus from their original purpose: the provision of a service for working parents. They reached their peak in the number of children attending during World War II. They now work with a very needy group of children, eligibility being restricted to those who are in some way vulnerable. The children who attend may be at risk of abuse, in need (physically, intellectually, emotionally, socially or behaviourally) or disabled (for a full definition see the Children Act (1989), Section 17 (10)). Funding comes from the Social Services budget, and though places are means-tested, in reality most parents pay nothing except the cost of meals.

The 'leader' of a day nursery is usually called the 'officer-in-charge', with 'nursery officer' as the term for other staff members. Everyone on the staff is likely to be qualified through the Nursery Nurses Examinations Board (NNEB). The system of training is changing, however, as the National Vocational Qualification (NVQ) and Business, Technical and Educational Certificate (BTEC) take over. All these qualifications, though, are based on a two-year course which is essentially practical, covering basic general preparation. The result may be that young people of only eighteen years are left in all-day charge of groups of children who have complex and demanding needs (Calder, 1995).

The premises of day nurseries are generally adequate (though poor and cramped in comparison with corresponding provision in most of Europe), and staff seem to give high priority to safety and hygiene. Equipment is generously provided, but often the emphasis is on bright plastic toys and construction sets and less on the more basic materials such as clay, paint, and equipment for water play and gardening activities. Considerable attention has been paid recently to ensuring that books, posters, puzzles, dolls, and so forth are representative of the cultural diversity of society in the United Kingdom.

Serious criticisms have been made about day nurseries, in particular relating to their intake policy and their lack of an educational ethos. A very disadvantaged group is typically created by bringing together solely children 'at risk' or 'in need' or from 'risky' home backgrounds – as where parents are on drugs, in prison, or deemed to be experiencing difficulty in bringing up their children. These children are thus deprived of the benefits of mixing with and learning from children who are free from such damaging circumstances. Children whose lives at home lack stability, order and positive experiences are the very ones who should ideally be in pre-school settings as life-enhancing as possible. But here lies the second problem. Day nurseries were set up to care for children over long periods (though nowadays few children attend full-time) but not to 'educate' them.

As we have seen they are staffed by people who have had only relatively short practical training. Many local authorities are attempting to achieve a more educational and creative environment, but a good solution remains to be found. In some areas trained nursery teachers have been seconded to day nurseries. Unfortunately this may cause resentment (in part due to the teachers' much more generous pay scale), but in any case teachers are not professionally trained for work with under-threes.

The number of day nurseries is not high and in some areas children are bussed in. This certainly reduces their contacts with their local community and may damage relationships. Furthermore there is a strong risk of stigmatisation for those who attend. Perhaps in the hope of reducing prejudice many day nurseries have changed their names and, to some extent, their roles. In their recent national survey Geva Blenkin and Nora Yue (1994) came across twelve different names for services pre-viously termed 'day nurseries', among them Family Centre, Under Fives' Resource Centre, Under Eights' Centre, Early Years' Centre. But while revising the name has often gone along with widening the scope of the service, the emphasis in these organisations still tends to be on supporting vulnerable children and not on providing a universal service (Stones, 1994).

Family centres

Regulated by:	social services department, occasionally education
Ages of children:	0–5 (may offer after-school care)
Ratio of adults to children:	1:3 (0–2-year-olds), 1:5 (2–5-year-olds)
Opening times:	variable.

Family centres are a relatively new concept, first mentioned in official legislation in the 1989 Children Act, although some had been in existence at least ten years earlier. All are registered by the social services department (apart from a very small number which are the responsibility of the local education authority (LEA)) but a considerable number are run and funded (sometimes in partnership with the local authority) by voluntary organi-sations, most notably the Save the Children, Barnados and the NCH Action for Children. In terms of cost to parents, these will be very low-cost or free. The original aims of family centres were to offer a varied and flexible set of activities to both children and adults, especially in disadvantaged localities. In practice they have developed different styles and a wide range of services including the informal 'drop-in' (for any parents with or without their children), playgroups, day-care facilities, 'special needs' groups, toy libraries, adult education and even clothes-washing facilities. Christine Stones' comprehensive research on family centres (1994) suggests that financial cutbacks are driving local authorities to use family centres more for work with children in difficulties, thus forcing centres away from their earlier principles of open access and a 'holistic' approach to children and families. On the other hand some have retained their community-based ethos and have democratically involved parents in the running of the centre. Among the 600 or so centres in the country there is great variety and it is hardly possible to portray a typical example. The report by June Statham of Save the Children five projects (1994) and Margy Whalley's study (1994) are also recommended for their informative and interesting accounts.

The challenge of finding appropriately trained staff for family centres, especially for the project leader or person-in-charge remains outstanding. There is no directly suitable qualification which covers all the specialised knowledge and skills required for work in at least three dimensions, with children, with parents and also the community. A very broad-based inter-disciplinary preparation is ideally demanded. At present, however, a Diploma in Social Work is the most likely qualification of leaders in family centres.

Nursery schools and classes

Regulated by:	local education authority
Ages of children:	3- and 4-year-olds
Ratio of adults to children:	1:10 in nursery schools, 1:13 in nursery classes
Opening times:	school terms and school hours; most children attend half time.

LEAs have at present no obligation to provide either nursery schools (in which all the children are of pre-school age) or nursery classes (in which the pre-school class is attached to an infant, first or primary school). Consequently their distribution across the country is very uneven. In some cities there are enough places for virtually every child to attend, whereas at the other extreme rural counties tend to provide very little or no nursery education.

Nursery schools and classes are required to be in the charge of a fully-trained teacher who must have either a four-year BEd degree or a three-year degree followed by a PGCE (postgraduate certificate of education). Along with the teacher each class will have one or two nursery assistants, usually qualified under the NNEB.

Almost a quarter of all three- and four-year-olds attend these types of pre-school which are free but almost always half-time – indeed, the morning or afternoon session may be quite brief, perhaps as little as two hours. Given the length of school holidays, the needs of working parents are far from being met. Parental involvement has much increased in nursery schools and classes, both in the form of day-to-day classroom help and through participation in governing bodies.

Traditional British nursery schools have had an international reputation for excellence and been an influential model in the development of pre-school curricula around the world. Their philosophy is distinctive and is based on the creation of a well-endowed, carefully planned environment in which each child is given personal responsibility to choose and carry out their own activities supported by well-informed and sensitive adults. The child's all-round development is the goal, but the underlying belief is that children can reach this goal through the powerful force of their individual intrinsic motivation. The nursery teacher and her (rarely his) assistant are trained in how to provide stimulating and challenging play activities through which children's learning takes place. *Just Playing?* (Moyles, 1989) gives a lucid account of education through play in the classroom.

In some parts of the United Kingdom the High/Scope curriculum is being used. This can be thought of as a development of the traditional nursery school with which it still has much in common. The most significant difference lies in the structuring of the child's thinking and time. On arrival in the nursery children *plan* what they intend to do or play with during the session. They then carry out their plan, they *do* what they have chosen, and finally towards the end of the session they *review* their activities in a small group with adult guidance. This cycle is known as *plan, do, review*. There is much interest in the High/Scope curriculum since very long-term research indicates that considerable social benefits accrue (Schweinhart *et al.*, 1993).

Independent private schools

Regulated by:	either the LEA or social services department
Ages of children:	3- and 4-year-olds
Ratio of adults to children:	variable, see below
Hours:	school terms and school hours.

A small but growing number of children attend private nursery schools or classes, which are invariably linked to independent preparatory or pre-preparatory schools. The registration of the school or class is the responsibility of either the social services department or the LEA, the defining criteria being whether children of statutory school age (five years old) are in the group. Where all the children are pre-schoolers the same rules apply as for playgroups, i.e. a ratio of 1:8. Should the group, on the other hand, have some children of school age, then 1:30 is required. Generally, though, class sizes are quite small. It is interesting to note that anyone can in theory set up a group and call it a 'school' and employ 'teachers' who are not qualified, but the registering authority will normally require the staff to have relevant experience and may insist on some form of training such as the NVQ. Parents will almost certainly find such schools an expensive option since they are often run for profit, yet they are chosen by some in the belief that the more formal style of teaching, typically found in independent private schools, is likely to benefit their child.

Playgroups

Regulated by:	social services departments
Ages of children:	2.5 years to 4 years
Ratio of adults to children:	1:8, in some areas 1:6
Opening times:	often 2 weekly sessions of 2–3 hours per child.

By far the majority of British children in their pre-school years attend playgroups. Playgroup history began in 1961 with a parent's letter to the *Guardian* newspaper arguing the need to provide play and social opportunities for children in the absence of nursery schools and suggesting that parents themselves should take the initiative. The writer was flooded with letters and in response the playgroup movement took off. Playgroups can now be found across the whole of the United Kingdom, though they are more common in rural areas. They seldom have exclusive use of premises and typically use village and church halls. Sometimes spare classrooms are available in schools, a few have their own purpose-built premises, and some are run in private houses. The adults leading playgroups come from many backgrounds. Almost always they will be parents themselves. Some may have teaching, nursing, or Nursery Nurses Examination Board training, but they are now more likely to have a playgroup course diploma (now the NVQ). It is essential to recognise that the playgroup course, though well-respected, is part-time and of a very different nature from the academic discipline of a four-year degree.

The playgroup leader and her assistant are usually paid (although at a very meagre rate) and will have other adults helping voluntarily – probably parents attending on a rota system. The parent helper and parental involvement in general are central principles of the playgroup movement. It was due to the energetic drive of many parents (largely, but not entirely women) during the 1960s and 1970s that playgroups mushroomed. These parents discovered that by 'doing-it-themselves' they gained in personal confidence and understanding. They learned a lot about children, about the crucial importance of 'play' and how best to promote it. They found out how to run a committee and manage finances, and how to negotiate with local authorities. Since then, however, the picture has changed since many women now expect to return to paid employment as soon as possible after their children are born. As a result the pool of voluntary helpers or parents prepared to work for very little money is drying up.

Because playgroups are part of the voluntary sector and receive very little public money, they have to charge parents fees in order to cover costs (of rent, heating, salaries, materials, etc.). Many groups are community-run charities but a few are private businesses, with the fees naturally reflecting the nature of the organisation.

Playgroups modelled themselves on the traditional nursery school and some provide children with a rich, well-equipped environment and are run by enthusiastic, sensitive adults. The range of quality is nevertheless very wide and sometimes the premises are far from adequate. The children may have to play on dubious village hall floors and to use possibly unhygienic adult toilets. The playgroup staff must sometimes carry equipment to and from an outside shed before and after a morning's play. In response to changing social patterns, some playgroups have begun to offer extended hours to cover the child care needs of employed parents, rather than the typical two mornings a week. With children possibly spending as much as eight hours a day in playgroups, for perhaps five days a week, the question of the physical surroundings becomes much more significant. Another new development is that, from February 1995, the Pre-school Playgroups Association (PPA) has changed its name to the Pre-school Learning Alliance – PLA – and is now encouraging its groups to re-name themselves 'pre-schools'. While the motive for change is said to be to 'remove ambiguity', and to indicate to parents that children will be learning from the playgroup curriculum (published by the PPA in 1991) 'tailored to the requirements' of the National Curriculum, this seems a huge change in emphasis away from the implicit principle of the value of play for all-round development. It remains to be seen how playgroups will evolve in consequence.

Parent and toddler groups

Regulated by:	no local authority involvement; often supported by PPA/PLA
Ages of children:	0–5 years
Ratio of adults to children:	none specified
Opening times:	one or two sessions (2–3 hours) per week.

These are very informal groups, not regulated in any official way since parents remain with their children all the time. On account of the lack of registration the number of parent and toddler (P/T) groups is unknown, but they are ubiquitous. Their aim is to offer a base for parents and children where they can all make social contacts while the children play in relaxed surroundings. All kinds of people looking after children make use of P/T groups, including childminders and nannies. This mutual support may be very important for more isolated carers and for those at risk of depression. The majority of children who attend are under three (after this age they usually 'graduate' to playgroups where they stay without their parents). Some mothers even attend P/T groups before their babies are born.

It is common for P/T groups to share the same premises as playgroups (church and village halls, for example), and sometimes they share even the equipment. The responsibility for running the P/T group is taken by volunteer helpers and the small fee which parents pay serves just to cover costs of rent, heat, refreshments and consumables. The number of adults and children present in the group at any session is very variable. It is possible to find, say, three or four parents with perhaps a total of four children, but other groups may have ten times that number.

Childminders

Regulated by:	social services department
Ages of children:	0 upwards
Ratio of adults to children:	1:3; this figure includes any young children the minder may have
Opening times:	full day throughout the year.

Childminder care is often the arrangement chosen for babies and children under two. Indeed this is frequently forced on parents because there is virtually no public provision for under-twos and very little in the private sector either. But even when group care is available, some families prefer the option of childminders. Not only do they offer a home-like atmosphere, but the small numbers of children present allow for more individual care as well as potentially more flexible personal arrangements for the parents.

Childminders are required by law to be registered with the social services department of the local authority if they are caring for a child (to whom they are not related) 'for reward' for more than two hours a day. There is concern that large numbers are still not registered. In deciding whether a childminder is suitable for registration the social services department looks at the quality of the person as well as the environment (health and safety, and available play equipment). The minder must be a 'fit' person, an assessment that includes ensuring that the minder is committed to equality of opportunity for all children whatever their gender, race, culture, language, religion, or possible disability. In other words the concept of 'fitness' covers not only material provision but non-discriminatory attitudes too.

Childminding has had a poor press in the past and probably occasional examples of bad practice can still be found. But where it is good it can be very good indeed. The National Childminding Association (NCMA) has played a most important role in raising the status and practice of childminders. Local support groups and training have given these potentially isolated workers the kind of backing, information and increased understanding which they need. There is still some way to go in ensuring that 'drop-in' centres, support and training groups are accessible to all minders and it is vital that childminders do not feel cut off. The final point to emphasise is an economic one. Childminding is rarely subsidised in the UK and is therefore quite an expensive option. On the other hand, from the point of view of the minder, if it is not paid for at a realistic rate then it exploits that worker.

Private nurseries

Regulated by:	social services department
Ages of children:	0–5 years
Ratio of adults to children:	1:3 (under two), 1:6 (2–5 years)
Opening hours:	full day throughout the year.

The private nursery offering full day care is something of a growth industry yet the demand for facilities that range from care for young infants to after-school care is still far from being met. Business firms (such as the Midland Bank), institutions (such as colleges, universities and hospitals) and private individuals are among those who organise services. They operate under all kinds of titles: crèches, kindergartens, nurseries, 'Tiny tots', 'Caterpillars' or whatever is fancied. Some are set up with an eye to profits, but if the provision is good and the staff properly recompensed, all at a cost that parents can reasonably afford, it is difficult to make much money. In terms of qualifications staff in nurseries are likely to have an NNEB certificate or possibly a PPA/PLA diploma, though some may have other backgrounds such as teaching. The private enterprise nurseries are extremely variable in quality. If some are excellent, others barely meet the criteria laid down in the Department of Health Guidelines. In one national study Jeni Vernon and Celia Smith (1994) found most children were apparently happy in their nurseries and that there were no cases of dangerous practice. All the same these researchers certainly give no cause for complacency. They suggest that staff needed much more training, especially in work with babies and in promoting children's learning through natural motivation and exploratory behaviour. Children's individual differences, their needs and wishes, were not always recognised, and the monitoring of individual progress was not given adequate attention. Staff were also insufficiently aware of anti-discriminatory issues and this was reflected in the lack of appropriate play equipment. Perhaps not surprisingly (since the parents were generally out at work) there was little parental involvement. A matter of greater concern was that parents had very low expectations of the style and quality of nurseries. It should be remembered too that children may spend very long hours in a nursery. Criticism of poor arrangements or lack of staff training is therefore serious.

Because private nurseries are expensive (sometimes exceedingly so) and because they are clearly not eligible for public funding, they tend to be used by people earning reasonably high salaries, rather than by the unemployed or poorer members of society.

Pre-school in Sweden: a comparative note

While most readers of this book will be observing children in the different British contexts described in this chapter, it is worth remembering that British practice has its limitations. Alternative systems can be found in many countries, some of them – it could be argued – superior to what is commonly regarded as acceptable in this country. Sweden is a case in point. There, local authorities are obliged by law to provide day care for the children of all parents who wish to use the service. Provision is available for children from their first birthday until they start statutory schooling at the age of either six or seven years. Before that, for the whole of a child's first year, either parent (father or mother) may take paid leave as of right. Virtually all parents take up this option, which allows time for a close relationship to develop between parent and child. In order to prevent parents feeling isolated during this year at home, and also to give the children group experiences, the Swedish local authorities provide *open pre-schools*, comparable in style to P/T groups in the UK and where parents stay with their children for the whole session. There the similarity ends, for the *open pre-schools* are located in purpose-built premises, well-equipped, and with staff qualified to degree level (through the three-year pre-school teachers' course). Most parents with children at home attend these *open pre-schools* every morning, having lunch there and then going home, though they are welcome to stay all day if they wish. Child minders also bring the children in their care to the *open pre-schools* where in some cases a day is set aside especially for them.

In addition to the rather informed *open pre-schools* (for parents and children together) there are also ordinary *pre-schools*, for children aged between one and seven years, open long hours to accommodate the children of any working parent (in Sweden 80% of women are in the labour force). The British visitor is impressed by these establishments. The well-designed, well-furnished buildings (sometimes attached to the primary school) have generous space both inside and out. Outdoor activity is given high priority, even in the cold Swedish winter, and almost always includes access to an area of woodland. The emphasis is on basic play activity, such as woodwork, cooking, building 'houses' in the wood, dramatic play, songs and stories. These activities are made possible by the high ratio of adults to children. As in the *open pre-schools* these adults will be graduates from pre-school teachers' courses. The philosophy of this professional group is notable for its strength and clarity. All pre-school teachers are committed to a developmental, child-centred style of working.

Longitudinal studies by Andersson (1989) have served to reassure those sceptics in Sweden who have been critical of any day care outside the home which separates children from their families. He has found the benefits of pre-school to be significant and long-lasting. Andersson himself, however, has recently admitted (1994) that the all-round experience of childhood in Sweden (including the particular context of housing, health services, welfare benefits, and the overall attitude towards children and families) makes it problematic to generalise from the Swedish experience and apply it unthinkingly elsewhere.

References and further reading

Andersson, B-E. (1989) 'Effects of public day care: A longitudinal study.' *Child Development 60*, 857–866.

Andersson, B-E. (1994) 'Public policies and early childhood education.' *European Early Childhood Education Research Journal 2*, 2, 19–32.

Blenkin, G. and Yue, N. (1994) 'Profiling early years practitioners: Some first impressions from a national survey.' *Early Years 15*, 1, 13–22.

Calder, P. (1995) 'New vocational qualifications in child care and education in the UK.' *Children and Society 9*, 1, 36–53.

Department of Health (1991) *The Children Act 1989 Guidance and Regulations, Volume 2 Family Support, Day Care and Educational Provision for Young Children.* London: HMSO.

Kumar, V. (1993) *Poverty and Inequality in the UK: the Effects on Children.* London: National Children's Bureau.

Moyles, J. (1989) *Just Playing? The Role and Status of Play in Early Childhood Education.* Milton Keynes: Open University Press.

Penn, H. and Riley, K. (1992) *Managing Services for the Under-Fives.* London: Longman.

Pugh, G. (1989) 'Services for under fives: current provision in context and a glossary of terms.' In S. Morgan and P. Righton (eds) *Child Care: Concerns and Conflicts*. London: Hodder and Stoughton and Open University.

Schweinhart, L.J., Barnes, H.V., and Weikart, D.P. (1993) *Significant Benefits: The High/Scope Perry Preschool Study Through Age 27*. Ypsilanti, Michigan: High Scope Press.

Statham, J. (1994) *Childcare in the Community*. London: Save the Children.

Stones, C. (1994) *Focus on Families: Family Centres in Action*. London: Macmillan in association with Barnados.

Vernon, J. and Smith, C. (1994) *Day Nurseries at the Crossroads: Meeting the Challenge of Child Care in the Nineties*. London: National Children's Bureau.

Whalley, M. (1994) *Learning to be Strong: Setting up a Neighbourhood Service for Under-fives and their Families*. London: Hodder and Stoughton.

CHAPTER FOUR

Observational Methods and Practice

Setting up an observation: recording methods

This chapter is intended to be highly practical and is designed especially to help students or practitioners make the most suitable choice of recording method for their purpose. Some kind of structured format is needed, rather than just a random and intuitive approach, but no format can be perfect and attention will be drawn to some of the relative strengths and limitations of the different methods described.

Your first task is to consider the reason why you are doing a series of observations at all. Student courses will almost certainly require observational work. The purpose might be to learn about children's development, to study some aspect of play (e.g. imaginative, fantasy play), or perhaps to focus on some process such as a child 'settling in to a new situation'. Observation within the day-to-day pre-school context may have different purposes – to explore why a child is causing concern, say, or to improve overall provision for children, or to investigate the different contexts in which a bilingual child uses one language or the other.

It will take time to become proficient and confident in using any method, and reflection on the process as well as discussion with colleagues, tutors or other students during the learning process can be very helpful. While many variations and adaptations are possible, the methods divide broadly into two groups: narrative methods and sampling methods. *Narrative methods* are those which simply attempt to record a slice of life in everyday language. They include Naturalistic Observation and the 'Tavistock method' which both have a very straightforward narrative format. There is also the Target Child method which is slightly more structured. Diary records, in which a more or less regular daily note is made, also belong in this group. This is the least structured of all methods. (You may enjoy *A Father's Diary* by Fraser Harrison, 1985.)

Sampling methods offer ways of making more selective observations, based either on time or events – hence their names, Time Sampling and Event Sampling. The Checklist method and Rating Scale, in which observation is restricted to watching for a pre-selected range of behaviours, are also of this type. Apart from the familiar diary record, each of these methods will be explained in detail below, giving actual examples as well as listing their strengths and limitations.

There are certain general points to note about observational studies which are applicable to whichever method you decide to use.

THE CHILD

A student observation must preserve the child's anonymity. For this reason only an initial, or a pseudonym, should be used. The child's gender and age should always be recorded. The usual practice in noting the age is to state the number of years and months separated by a colon, so that for 3 years 10 months you write 3:10. You should also note the child's home language.

THE OBSERVATION

The time of day will need to be noted as well as the date of the observation, since this may indicate whether the child is fresh or tired.

THE SETTING

Before beginning the observation those aspects of the environment which might affect the child's behaviour should be summarised. You should note down the number of adults and of children present, the play opportunities for the children, and what, if anything, the children are expected to be doing at the time of the observation (e.g. sitting listening to a story, or free play). This will take a few minutes and should give you time to tune into a possibly quite complex atmosphere, with many lively children.

1. Naturalistic Observation

This narrative method is sometimes called 'specimen description', 'written record', or 'running record'. Since it is by far the simplest method, structured only by noting the sequence of time, it may be the best one to start with. Observers must write down (on the spot) as much as they can of what they are seeing. This will normally be written in ordinary longhand, although it is a good idea to adopt simple abbreviations where possible, for example A for any adult, LH and RH for left and right hand, and so on. The present tense is used, and at one-minute intervals the time is noted in a margin ruled on the left-hand side of the paper. The only materials required are thus paper, pen or pencil, and a watch (preferably one showing seconds). An observation of twenty minutes will seem quite demanding until you become accustomed to the intense concentration required.

Naturalistic Observation: example

Date: 17/2/95	Time: 09.35
Child's initial: D	Gender: M.
Age: 2:8	Date of Birth: 13.6.92
Child's home language:	English
Setting:	Nursery, free play – water tray, play dough, jigsaw puzzles, children's books.
Number and age of children:	14 (2–4 year-olds)
Number of adults:	4
Activity:	Adults tidying up and encouraging children to go and sit on carpet for a story.

TIME	
9.35	D 'spooning' water with small cup into saucepan. Bending over water tray, his bottom slightly stuck out, seems slightly awkward.
9.36	A 'Go and sit on the carpet'. D keeps on water play.
9.37	A (in firm voice) 'Come and sit down D'. D, pulling up trousers, walks slowly over and sits down quietly with other children. A starts to read story. D looks at me.
9.38	D sits very still, doesn't move though he can't see the pictures properly.
9.39	Hunches up shoulders, continues to sit very still, seems to be listening very carefully.
9.40	At sight of picture of plate of biscuits says 'Bistets'. Then 'The cat wants a bistet'. A acknowledges D with 'Yes, D, the cat wants a biscuit'.

Some researchers have modified this method by using a tape-recorder in place of a note-pad. They quietly dictate their description into the microphone, transcribing the recording at a later stage. Alternatively, tape-recordings of children's actual conversations can be made. These can capture the immediacy and detail of children's conversation. Blind students in particular have employed the technique with success, by taping children's play in relatively small rooms. They could then re-run the tape at home and analyse it in detail. Students should note, however, that in a lively pre-school environment, possibly in a large echoing hall, good sound quality is not always easy to achieve.

ADVANTAGES

- ° requires no advance preparation (but remember pen, paper and watch)

- ° feels 'natural' (easy to get started)

- ° picks up everything without selection (as a video camera would)

- ° creates all-round picture of the child, the complexity of behaviour

- ° records the 'ecology' of the environment.

LIMITATIONS

- ° creates dilemmas as to what and how much to record

- ° produces a mass of unstructured data

- ° lumps all kinds of information together

- ° makes it difficult to compare observations.

2. Target Child Method

The origins of this style of recording can be traced back to the methods used in the study of animals by ethologists (see Chapter Two). The actual Target Child method was developed by Kathy Sylva and her colleagues during the 1970s as a tool for investigating pre-school children's behaviour, in particular to study children's powers of concentration and the circumstances which promote this. That study was part of the Oxford Pre-school Research Project and, ever since its publication, the method has continued to be used by both students and practitioners in varied situations. Basically it is a straightforward technique using a simple pre-coding system for collecting data. A little advance preparation is required in the form of drawing up a grid on which to record the observation, and deciding on suitable abbreviations. A full description can be found in Appendix A of Sylva, Roy and Painter (1980), but the essential information needed to use the method is given below.

Date:	Time:	Child's Initial:	Gender:
Age:	Date of Birth:	Setting:	

Activity Record	Language Record	Task	Social
1.			
2.			
3.			
4.			
5.			
6.			
7.			
8.			
9.			
10.			

Figure 4.1. Target Child recording sheet (shown here at reduced size)

Target Child: example

Date: 1.3.95   Time: 10.01   Child's Initial: P   Gender: M
Age: 2:8   Date of Birth: 13.6.92
Setting: Nursery, free play (jigsaws, dressing-up, painting, etc.).
                  8 children, 2 adults. One A with large cardboard boxes,
                  tubes and big cardboard cable reels (like wheels)

Activity Record	Language Record	Task	Social
1. P picks up tube in RH. Bashes cardboard reel with it	C > P, You're breaking it. A > C, No, he's not. Those are for making it. P makes whacking noises		
2. Stands very still, watching other children and listening. Almost in a dream-like state	A explains about making a caravan for children to sit in, using boxes and spools.		
3. Watches A and three children arranging boxes and wheels for caravan. Hands on hips	A > P, What could that bit be for P? P, I don't know		
4. Watching closely, kneels down. Puts tube in box. Takes it out. A gives P end of strong, wide sellotape	A > P, Can you help me? A > P, Will you hold that? Can you pull on this?		
5. Starts to pull tape, it's too hard for him. Grits teeth, look of determination	A > P, Keep on pulling P A (explains how they are making caravan)		
6. Pushes roll of tape back along top of box (A guides him). Other children push and shove around	A > P, Where does it go this time? P, That way? A > P, Let someone else have a go		

Activity Record (continued)	Language Record (continued)	Task	Social
7. Walks slowly away. Looks at jigsaw table and children there. Wanders to alphabet chart on wall			
8. Returns to group making caravan. Picks up one reel, takes it away, and then another, making a pile away from the construction	A > P, Can you bring them over here?		
9. Puts reels one by one in big box (caravan). Carries last one to boy lying down	P, There's a wheel for you C, Thank you		
10. Wanders back to caravan construction. Takes another wheel to lying down boy, smiling broadly	Laughs with funny squeaky gleeful sound.		
11.			
12.			

The design of the recording sheet (or grid) is shown in Figure 4.1. A watch, ideally one showing seconds, will be required so that you can record minute by minute both the activity and the language used. Each number on the sheet represents one minute. The abbreviations suggested will help to speed up note-taking, but of course you can create your own.

TC = target child (the one you are observing)

C = any other child

A = any adult (a member of staff, a parent helper, another student, or you)

> = speaks to

In the *ACTIVITY RECORD* column you write down *what the child does* within each minute-period, while in the *LANGUAGE RECORD* column you record verbatim *everything the child says*. You can also add conversation directed towards the target child in the *LANGUAGE* column, e.g. A > TC 'Come and have your drink', or A > TC (about going to the toilet). The other two columns are normally used once the observation is completed. The first (labelled *TASK*) is based on the actual task the child was engaged on – e.g. painting, music – which may be noted using letter codes. (This coding is useful if the purpose of the observation is to study specific pre-school activities. *TASK* coding is set out in the Appendix of this book.) The final column (labelled *SOCIAL*) affords an opportunity to pick out from the record the types of social contacts the child was engaging in, whether playing alone, in parallel, in a small or large group (see section on Social development and cultural context in Chapter Five). Twenty minutes is a suitable length of time to observe, though you may like to start with ten minutes and build up to the longer time span. Do not worry if you are interrupted for any reason. Simply write 'Interruption' and resume as soon as you can.

ADVANTAGES

- needs only basic preparation of grid
- focuses observation by use of simple grid structure, which also aids later analysis
- is flexible and open-ended.

LIMITATIONS

- ° takes a little practice to become proficient with the method
- ° requires some preparation
- ° constrains some observers by imposing a grid structure.

3. 'Tavistock Method'

Since 1948 a distinctive model of infant observation has been used as part of the training of child psychotherapists, originally at the Tavistock Clinic in London but subsequently elsewhere. The focus of this type of study is the early development of an infant (from soon after birth) in the family home, with the observer making an observation lasting one hour, every week, for two years. In this method students record, *after* the visit, as much as possible of the detail of what they have seen. Students attend weekly seminars with a leader, in small groups (typically of five members) at which they present, in turn, observations of 'their' babies. The aim of the study is 'to describe the development of the relationship between infant and others, including the observer, and to try to understand the unconscious aspects of behaviour and patterns of communication' (Miller *et al.*, 1989, p.7). The observations are recorded in 'literal everyday, untheorised language' (p.74), but the foundation of the whole approach is psychoanalytic theory, with the impact on the observer being regarded as of considerable importance. 'Emotion holds a cardinal place; it has to be observed and recorded and it will occur in the observer and the reader. It is not a distraction or a contaminant. Correctly grasped, the emotional factor is an indispensable tool to be used in the service of greater understanding' (p.3).

Certain social work course programmes use adaptations of this method even though it does pose problems (see the 'limitations' listed after the example below). On the other hand, used as the focus for a course at post-qualifying level for those working intensively with damaged and vulnerable children and their families, it does provide a valuable learning approach.

Tavistock Method: example

'Andrew is the second of two children; his older brother was two and a half when he was born. His parents, both in their early thirties, are a well-educated, middle-class couple...'.

Observation at three weeks

At the first observation, mother had much to say after our initial exchanges: 'Luckily he sleeps a lot, even at night; my first child was always awake during the night. It was terrible! At the moment he is not sleeping really deeply because of his cold; I have a cold too. Sometimes the baby seems old and tired, and so bored!' With a voice full of concern she continued, 'Sometimes I put him on my bed so that he has something more to look at', and later, 'This baby is luckier than the other because now, with the other child around, there is always noise in the house. His brother often puts his face very, very near to the baby's face, smiling at him. That is wonderful for the baby, and adults never do that.' (Miller *et al.* 1989 p.118)

ADVANTAGES

- ° requires only simple materials
- ° uses everyday language
- ° creates a detailed picture of the child
- ° includes adult interaction
- ° allows developmental changes to be seen over a long period of observation.

LIMITATIONS

- ° demands accurate recollection *after* the visits
- ° depends on a very long time commitment
- ° focuses strongly on baby–adult interaction
- ° is limited to the period of early infancy
- ° concentrates to a large extent on emotional development
- ° starts from a particular theoretical perspective.

4. Time Sampling

The observational methods so far described all involve a narrative, 'story-telling' style. They give a picture of the child's behaviour in context and in enough detail to understand what was taking place. Moreover, the original order of the events is maintained. However, recording in a narrative fashion creates large amounts of data which may be difficult to analyse.

Time sampling provides a way of recording which concentrates on a selected aspect of behaviour in order to discover its frequency patterns. As a method it originated in the United States during the 1920s for the purpose of studying children in the laboratory nursery schools then being established. The nervous habits of normal children was the topic of the first time-sampling study, but the best-known was Mildred Parten's study of children's play (see Irwin and Bushnell, 1980, p. 148). Time sampling is suited only to behaviour which can actually be observed (day dreaming as a topic is therefore out) and which can be described in clear terms. The behaviour patterns must occur reasonably frequently (at least every fifteen minutes) so that they can be recorded in a relatively short period of time.

The purpose of the study must first be thoroughly worked out. If, for example, the aim is to examine the strategies by which a child obtains adult attention then preliminary observations will be necessary in order to identify the range of possible behaviours. These might be verbal – calling out or asking politely for help; or non-verbal – tapping or pulling the adult; or perhaps indirect – disturbing other children with the purpose of attracting attention. These behaviours must be detailed precisely so that they can easily be identified during the observation session. In effect this means devising a kind of checklist (further discussed in the section on the Checklist Method later in this chapter).

A second kind of time sampling might also be tried. In this case it is a child's *total* behaviour, not *selected* behaviour, that is under investigation. It is a useful technique for discovering just what a child typically does throughout a day, or what kinds of social contacts she/he regularly has. For this technique the timing needs to be planned in three ways: first, the total amount of time available has to be decided on; next, the length of the time unit for observation; and, finally, the intervals between the observational units. So, for instance, in one morning a child might be observed for one minute every fifteen minutes. The observer would note

Time Sampling: example
TOPIC: Getting adult attention

The playgroup leader is concerned about M, a boy aged 3.6. She believes that he is making excessive demands on the adults, and wishes to find out how frequently this really is happening and what types of behaviour he is using. Having identified the range of strategies he tends to use, she has grouped them as follows:

Verbal attention-seeking: *acceptable* forms include:
'Please may I...?, 'I'd like...', or addresses the adult by name.

Verbal attention-seeking: *undesirable* forms include:
'Give me...' (in very demanding tones), swearing, screaming and shouting out very loudly.

Non-verbal attention-seeking: *acceptable* behaviour includes:
taps or pats adult, looks into her face and stands right in front of her.

Non-verbal attention-seeking: *undesirable* behaviour includes:
pulling the adult roughly by her arm or clothes, pushing or punching her.

PLAN FOR OBSERVATION

The adult decides to watch for one minute at 15-minute intervals and to record the observations by ticking in the appropriate column.

Date: Time: 9.00 am.   Child:
Gender: Age: Home language:
Activity:

Language and Behaviour		Time				
		9.15	9.30	9.45	10.00	etc.
Verbal:	acceptable					
	undesirable					
Non-verbal:	acceptable					
	undesirable					

(*An analysis and bar chart based on this example is given Chapter Five.*)

Time Sampling: example 2
TOPIC: Study of book corner

Books have regularly been found scattered around the room at the end of the morning session. None of the adults is sure how this has happened.

PLAN OF OBSERVATION

Every 15 minutes the observer will briefly note down the names of children in the area of the book corner, and what they are doing there.

Date: Starting Time: 9.00
Activity: Book corner

Time	Children	What is happening
9.00	Kim and Ross	Gathering books into piles on carpet, laughing and chattering.
9.15	Raj	Sitting quietly, looking at pictures in alphabet book.
9.30	Kim and Ross	Trying to climb on book-shelves, giggling.
9.45	Kim, Ross and Winston	Replacing a few books on the shelves, Winston telling the others what to do.
etc.		

---

down in the one-minute observation period the child's activity (where she is and what she is doing), what she is saying, and who she is with.

A third way of using time sampling, is to focus on some activity (such as the book corner) and to spend one minute every fifteen minutes (or other convenient time span) noting which children are in the activity area and what they are doing. The temptation, of course, is to go on watching beyond the defined minute, particularly if something interesting is happening. This must be resisted!

ADVANTAGES

- gathers precise, focused information
- collects a large amount of data in a relatively short period of time
- records information that is easily understood
- allows the fine grain of a particular behaviour to be studied
- allows comparisons to be made (e.g. of children of different ages)
- sometimes reveals unsuspected patterns of behaviour.

LIMITATIONS

- demands accurate time-keeping (over possibly a whole morning) which may be difficult
- collects fragmentary information
- merely samples behaviour which may be unrepresentative
- studies only overt and frequent behaviours
- is unsuitable for investigating such topics as imaginative play
- does not reveal why certain behaviours occur
- fails to examine the quality of experiences
- pre-determines observation, so risking bias and potential neglect of important behaviour.

5. Event Sampling

The perennial problem with all observation is how to deal with large quantities of data generated by the complex activity which has been observed. Whereas time sampling, as we have seen, selects data from the stream of events, event sampling selects by concentrating on a particular short period of behaviour. It is helpful in investigating such episodes as quarrels, say, or in looking at a child's problem-solving behaviour within a defined period. Other suitable topics for event sampling might be tidying-up sessions, meal-times, or an activity like listening to a story. The unit of observation is the event itself, which may be of any length. While it is unwise to attempt to observe for too long a period, the actual observation time cannot be decided in advance. In preparation it is necessary to identify clearly the aspect of behaviour or topic you are

interested in and exactly what information you are after. In the ca
quarrel, you may want to know how long it lasted, what was happ   g
before it began, who was involved, what they said and did, what brought
the quarrel to a conclusion and what the outcome was. With this technique
it is usual to recommend the preparation of a recording sheet in advance
so that you can jot down information rapidly, but you will also need space
for a narrative description, just as with the Naturalistic Description method
outlined earlier. The moment to start systematic observation is when you

---

Event Sampling: example
TOPIC: Frequency and type of play between D and W

D is new in the group and still unsure of himself. Often he seems to be
playing with W (a year older) who is very excitable (perhaps even
hyperactive). Staff feel that D is getting into trouble because of W's
leadership.

Date: 6.2.95   Starting Time: 9.00
Activity: Free play

Number	Time and Length	Event
1.	9.15 (1 minute)	W > D 'Let's play picnics'. They rush into home corner, grabbing bags and pretend food. Take it to the climbing frame. D drops everything he is carrying and joins adult at craft table.
2.	9.45 (5 minutes)	D joins W at climbing frame saying, 'There's a fire'
		W shouts, 'Get everything out!' They throw everything out (they had collected clothes, jigsaws, etc.). A 'Calm down, let's put it all away.'
		W and D lie down inside the climbing frame and refuse to come out, etc.

see the event begin. You note the time and continue to watch until the episode is concluded.

- ° suits any reasonably short, defined event
- ° helps in defining and understanding problems
- ° aids later analysis since the 'event' itself forms the structure
- ° potentially reveals cause and effect.

- ° requires an alert, available observer to pick up the cue of an imminent event
- ° produces data lacking the clarity of Time Sampling
- ° may lead to less objective observation since behaviours are predefined.

6. Checklist Method

The checklist is a very familiar tool, for shopping, jobs to be done, and so on. In the context of observation it is simply a list of behaviours deemed to be important, which can be ticked off as and when they are noted. Checklists are commonly used for recording stages of development in health, education and other areas, and examples can easily be found (see Drummond *et al.*, 1992, for details about the Portage project and Playladders). Some local education authorities use them at the point their four-year-olds enter school to pick up information about physical, cognitive, social and emotional development. Checklists, though, cannot take the place of true observation. They are better thought of as summaries of observations.

In the section on Time Sampling one type of checklist was described, and there the items were linked to frequency of occurrence. The preparation for the checklist method obviously includes the preliminary creation of an actual list. Target behaviours have to be selected, defined precisely, and the list organised logically (typically from the simple to the more complex).

Check List: example
TOPIC: Focus: Four-year-olds' knowledge of some basic concepts

---

Tick or circle as preferred.

1. *Shapes:* can identify the following:

> circle
> square
> triangle

2. *Colours:* can identify the following:

> red
> blue
> yellow
> etc.

Dates and other details may be added.

A *Rating Scale* is another kind of checklist where an aspect of behaviour is considered and then judged, or 'rated', for location at some point on a scale. A five-point scale is very commonly adopted. The advantage of the Rating Scale over the basic checklist is that it grades the level of response rather than confining it to a simple yes or no.

Rating Scale: example
TOPIC: Co-operation

Tick the statement most closely corresponding to the observed behaviour.

1. Very keen to work/play with others

2. Seems to like working/playing with others

3. Works/plays satisfactorily

4. Mostly works/plays alone

5. Never works/plays with others.

ADVANTAGES

- is simple to use, once the list is constructed
- uses the observer's time and energy efficiently
- produces records that are easy to read and understand
- shows immediately what a child can and cannot do
- notes behaviours as soon as they occur
- assists making comparisons e.g. of age or gender.

LIMITATIONS

- depends entirely on the soundness of the checklist
- may include trivia because easy to observe and 'tick off'
- gives no information about quality of behaviour
- does not reveal reasons for behaviour
- poses risk of observer-subjectivity creating biased resuts.

Setting up an observation: contacting a pre-school group and selecting a child

The circumstances in which observations take place are extremely varied and this textbook is attempting to offer guidance across many possible situations. Those who work with young children, as part of their day-to-day responsibilities, will have their own reasons for undertaking observations, some of which have already been mentioned. Students on a course are, by contrast, in a very different position and may have to find children to study. Most of this section is targeted at the needs of students rather than pre-school personnel.

The earlier chapter on pre-school services gives a certain amount of background information which should help. Obviously it is a good idea to seek out, if possible, some pre-school group within easy reach in your own locality. You may be surprised to discover many pre-school groups, such as parent-and-toddler groups, crèches and playgroups, sometimes meeting in unlikely venues. Your greatest difficulty might be finding one open at a time when you yourself are available. As a general rule it is better to go to a group that offers a 'universal' service, in other words a group open to all children and not confined to those who attend primarily for therapeutic reasons. A neighbourhood community group or some kind of nursery (work-place, school or class – see Chapter Three) should all accept a cross-section of children and prove a suitable choice. The reason for this advice is that where the majority of children have been referred, perhaps by social workers, they and their family will be subjects of special concern and scrutiny. In these circumstances it may be better not to add more surveillance by yet another adult. Among the first things you should check is whether the group has students already, perhaps like you engaged on observations, and whether it can still comfortably accommodate you.

A letter of introduction, explaining the purpose of the observation task and what is expected of the pre-school group, should already have been made available for the student to give to the leader. Most groups are remarkably generous with their hospitality towards students, recognising that this is a vital part of the process of learning about children. Setting up an observation offers an interesting experience in communication. The letter of introduction is only the preliminary to a fuller explanation of the observation project. It is essential to cover such aspects as the number of visits the student intends, their timing and duration, and the purpose of them (probably to do with improving observation skills and learning about child development). Finally it is important to reassure those working in the group that the observations will not be in any way judgemental or reflect critically on the group itself. Their object is solely to facilitate student learning. Confidentiality will be maintained throughout, all participants being treated in the observation record as anonymous and unidentifiable. The request to observe will obviously be made in such a way that the leader of the group can easily refuse. Again permission will need to be sought from the parent(s), who must also feel able to turn down the proposal without loss of face. Pre-school leaders are usually very helpful in assisting contact between the parents and the student.

Being present as an observer in a group brings into focus several significant issues. Students will not wish to be too conspicuous (e.g. in dress) as a visitor, to avoid attracting unnecessary attention and so affect the observation. More important, they must take into account their own race, class and gender in relation to the majority of the group, staff, parents and children. The white male in a largely female, ethnically mixed group will inevitably have a different impact from, say, a black woman in the same group. However well-meaning, self-effacing and anti-racist we believe ourselves to be, we may still appear to others, through our class, the language we use, and our personal style to represent negative, prejudiced, and even oppressive attitudes in society. It is notoriously difficult to empathise with other people's life experiences, for we cannot get inside another person's skin. Nevertheless it is vital to recognise and acknowledge the power structures that do exist. Disability raises some of the same issues, as does gender orientation. It is to be hoped that course programmes will give students ample opportunity for in-depth study of all anti-discriminatory matters. The topic is raised here because you may not realise the kind of power you have as a seemingly lowly student-observer. In your choice of which child to study you will need to be aware of the risk of stereotyping and of prejudice hampering your objectivity, especially if you decide on a child from a culture other than your own. Equally there are risks in choosing a child whom you assume to be very much of your own class and culture (perhaps even imagining this child to be a replica of yourself at that age). In the end you may be surprised how far this child differs from you. The importance of an open mind cannot be emphasised too strongly. Students who are also parents are advised to select a child of a different age from their own, if at all possible, in the interests of objectivity.

The last step in setting up an observation may involve getting the child's permission. Should you obtain agreement from the child first? There is no question that the child's rights should be of first importance. Whatever form observation takes, it must be ethical and respectful of the individual. Much depends on the child's age and ability to understand a simple explanation on the lines of 'I'd like to come and see the the sort of work and play you do'. Furthermore, some would argue that by seeking the child's consent the observer may cause self-consciousness, acting-up or distorted behaviour. Perhaps the best test, remembering that children are very aware of what is happening although they may not necessarily talk about it, is to ask yourself what you would have felt in those circumstances yourself. As with adults, if children are to be asked, they must have a genuine chance to say no. Finding the language to put this request to a young child may be quite a challenge, especially for a student unfamiliar with that age-group.

Carrying out an observation

The role of observer needs careful consideration since it is likely to be different from any other roles you are familiar with. In some ways it may feel unnaturally passive, although in reality it is mentally demanding. New observers indeed often find the intense concentration tiring. Your aim, whatever the form of recording chosen, is to absorb and note as much of the behaviour of your chosen child as you can. You are there in order to take in information, not to respond or to act. This is best achieved by being as unobtrusive as possible, endeavouring to make your physical movements so quiet and undemonstrative that you do not attract attention. If convenient, sit near to the action. If you have to stand, maintain an attentive stillness. You will have come prepared with recording sheets or notebook, pens and a watch, but wait for at least ten minutes before starting the observation. Use this adjustment period to absorb the atmosphere and to start making sense of a potentially very lively scene. Meanwhile the basic facts about numbers of adults and children, available materials, and the structure of activities in progress can all be noted down. When you are ready to begin the observation, check the time, then off you go, giving the task your full attention. Sometimes it is easy to be side-tracked, perhaps by another child, but be as self-disciplined as you can. While performing the observation it is better to avoid eye-contact with your subject because children will almost certainly attempt to draw you into their play.

Some common problems

When adults in pre-school settings are unused to student observers they may need some help in understanding what is involved. In the first place, as an observer you will prefer an ordinary, everyday session, in which there are no special arrangements either for you or for the child being observed. You want everyone to continue as normal, as if no observer were present. Secondly, the purpose of your visit is merely to observe, not to assist or look after the children if someone happens to be called away. Nor is this a social visit – so the observer may have to avoid being drawn into general conversation. Students may be surprised to find themselves being put in the role of expert and asked for advice. All these dilemmas can be dealt with in a friendly but firm way. Much more worrying is handling a situation which causes you, as on-looker, personal concern. Perhaps you feel that children are not being treated with respect or that the child care is unsatisfactory. You may overhear racist or sexist remarks. It is difficult to give general advice, but as a visitor with a specific role, that of observer, you should intervene only if there is immediate physical danger. Your position is that of the 'good citizen'. When you do have unresolved anxieties it is best to raise them with your course tutor or possibly (while continuing to ensure anonymity) to discuss the issues in a seminar group.

Yet another scenario might present itself. The child you are observing, or another child in the group, may try to interrupt you. They may be curious (especially if you have not chosen to explain your presence). They may ask what you are doing, sometimes trying to tempt their observer into a game by making enticing remarks, such as, 'Does this tiger go in this hole? Oh no, he doesn't, that one's for the lion!'. Some may engage in 'stagey' behaviour in an attempt to capture your interest. Such interest and curiosity are normal, natural behaviour, for young children gain a great deal from interaction with the more experienced members of their community (and this includes people like you, students). They have an almost insatiable appetite for involvement and conversation with adults. If they cannot draw an adult into their activities by low-key, more-or-less sophisticated methods, some children adopt tactics which are less accept-able or even dangerous. What in that case should you do? Prevention is, in my view, better than cure. Try to avoid getting involved. Try to appear boring, not much fun. The children may then ignore you. Should they ask you, 'What are you doing?' it is best to answer honestly: 'I'm writing about the children's play.'

As already mentioned, you may become aware of the risk of an accident, a situation in which a child could possibly be hurt, and which no other adult seems to have noticed. Only then might you justifiably, and sensibly, step in.

Observation in a home setting

Some courses require students to make one or more home visits as part of a child study. Observation in a private home is bound to be different from a group setting with perhaps twenty or more children and several adults. The observer is now without doubt in a very different relationship with both child(ren) and adult(s). Greater empathy and respect will be needed, for this is not a public, community facility, but a private and very personal world. You might, as an observer, feel that this is an intrusive activity and even that it is not appropriate. Visits to homes on child observation can be viewed in another way though, and those tutors and organisations which have experience of home-visiting back this up in their research findings. For the most part parents truly welcome genuine interest in their child and her or his development. Given the chance, the majority of parents will talk freely, and even with pleasure, about their child's history and interests. Our British society tends not to be very tolerant of parents who talk about their child's achievements, which may explain why it is usually easy to engage parents in conversation about their offspring. The essential points to convey to parents are that the child being studied is respected and valued, and that the student appreciates the insights and information gained from interviewing the parents and observing the child. Every child is unique and every study built up in this way is similarly unique.

Conclusion of a series of observational visits

As you near the end of the series of visits it is worth giving some thought as to how you wish to conclude them. This applies even to a relatively short observation programme. Apart from the more obvious aspects, such as expressing thanks and ensuring your hosts know that this will be your final day with them, it should also be an opportunity to confirm that they understand what you intend doing with all those notes you have diligently been making. The observations belong to the student. They are purely study materials and there is no obligation to show them either to the parents or staff.

Evaluation of observational visits

For the sake of clarity I propose to look at the analysis of raw observational data in the next chapter. There you will find suggestions about themes to explore and ways of sharing your findings with other people. The section which now follows offers instead some ideas about how to evaluate the process of observation itself. For a series of observational visits to become more than just a simple means of gathering information, indeed for the process to be truly a learning experience, it is necessary to reflect subsequently on what occurred in a thoughtful, critical way. Observation will continue to be an important tool in our work and it is worth giving time at this stage to grasping the obvious mechanics of what happens during observation as well as considering the more subtle, hidden processes at work. You may also find, as I personally do even after many years' experience, that insights into facets of human behaviour can be achieved through observational study that might not otherwise occur. But this will only come about if you maintain a critical and questioning stance. Ideally you should have the opportunity for discussion in small seminar groups with others engaged in similar observational work. You should then benefit from the discoveries of your fellow students, compare your individual findings with theirs, and share perspectives on the many issues likely to be raised. A group can also provide sympathetic support if this is needed. (The final chapter of this book discusses further the role of the seminar group.)

Even with great foresight, planning and good fortune it is unlikely that your observational visits will have gone perfectly. Even if you feel they have been highly successful, some reflection on the reason for this is in order. Those undertaking observations as part of a course programme will in any case almost certainly be asked to evaluate the process. This section should help you to structure your evaluation. But first, what should be evaluated? In my view there are two broad areas: the actual process and technique of observing, and the impact of the observations on all the people involved – the child, the workers in the group visited, the parents and, not least, the observer.

The process and technique of observation

How did you manage? What did you find difficult? Was it hard to capture *all* the behaviour you saw? Could you write fast enough? Did your notes make sense afterwards? One likely reason for possible dissatisfaction with your actual recording technique is simply that you have not yet become adept. As with any skill, regular practice makes all the difference, and you may just have needed more time. Students may not realise the problems faced by tutors in designing course programmes. Because there is usually far more curriculum to be covered than can reasonably be managed, important components like observation skills practice may not be allocated the time they deserve. It may therefore be a matter of offering just enough of a topic to serve as an introduction to the field. So it is important to pay regard to your own progress, and to compare your abilities on your first observation visit and later on. Are you becoming quicker and more fluent in recording? Rest assured that you will speed up in time, know better what is significant to record, and find the words coming more easily to describe the events happening so rapidly before you.

By using this book you should have made a careful choice of which technique to use. Now is the time to consider whether it was appropriate for your task. How well did it work for you? What did you like or dislike about it? Was it easy and straightforward? Would you make any modifications for a similar future task? These methods are not sacred 'tablets of stone' and are always being adapted by researchers and practitioners to suit individual needs.

The impact on the individuals involved: the child

You need to consider the effect your presence had on the child you were observing and whether your subject knew who you were and what you were doing? You should ponder whether the child's play was altered in any way by your being there and to what extent your presence might have affected the group dynamics. The smaller the group the more likely and stronger your impact was. These questions are not raised to suggest that you should have had *no* effect, but to alert you to the fact that any visitor (especially one coming for several weeks) does make a difference, and that the difference is most often positive. Children in their years before school learn at a dramatic rate; they are inquisitive about *everything*. They seek out new experiences and ideas, and you, the visiting observer, are one of these fresh experiences. Many examples have been given to me of the pleasure that individual pre-school children, especially boys, take in having a male visitor to their group. The reason for this is probably that in the world of under-fives contacts with men are sometimes few and far between. Staffing in pre-school groups rarely includes men (a topic discussed in Chapter Two) and single-parent households, of which there are increasing numbers, are largely led by women. Children may also welcome with pleasure someone of their own race – though it is a reflection on the distortions caused by racism in our society that a black child may not always feel comfortable with a visitor of her or his own colour.

Should you happen to be a student observer with a visible disability, the child(ren) may well be curious and ask questions which among older people would sound impertinent. At this stage in children's lives this questioning attitude is essential. They must learn, and you can help. In one instance a visually impaired student, with a guide dog, was regarded as a welcome and interesting visitor, and the children greatly benefited from his periodic calls to tape-record their conversation and play.

All the same, while your presence as a visitor may well be a source of interest for some children, it is possible you may unsettle others. Whatever the case, do not assume that because they have not referred to you they are unaware of your presence. But children learn very rapidly what appears to be the *status quo*. If you keep a very low profile, hardly make any eye-contact, and speak only to the person-in-charge, then your target child may come to disregard you entirely, even treating you like a piece of furniture. The explanation for this is that from the very start you have set up the expectation that you are not in any way available and that your role is not of interest to the children.

The impact on the individuals involved: the adults in the group

Pre-school groups have a host of different adults associated with them. In a parent-and-toddler group all the parents will be present as well as the leaders, while the health visitor or social worker may call in from time to time. Playgroups, nursery schools and classes almost all have volunteer helpers in addition to paid staff. You may also frequently find other students on placement or making child studies. You can see already that the impact you have on other adults in these busy places may well be marginal, since to them you may seem just part of the normal routine. Nevertheless the student observer, notebook in hand, can arouse anxiety and even suspicion. People working in pre-school settings, like anyone else, want others to think well of them. Faced by a student observer they may feel they are being assessed and in consequence try to raise the level of their performance. Recently a student reported that the staff in the nursery where she was observing re-organised the whole morning's activities to accommodate her, possibly because of the student's failure to make clear she wanted to observe the child in a normal morning's programme. Still, it is worth bearing in mind that most of the adults leading pre-school groups or classes will have carried out child observations themselves, as part of their training, and hence will be very understanding and supportive.

The impact on the individuals involved: the parent(s)

In reflecting on the effect of the planned observations, the life-style and cultural traditions of the family cannot be ignored. There is not just one stereotypical family even within any one social class. The observer should guard carefully against making assumptions about what the parent(s) might think. Instead listen carefully to what they say and observe non-verbal clues. There is another set of variables to take into account. Your observational programme may range, on the one hand, from little or no personal involvement with the parents (other than a letter of agreement) to the regular weekly visits, over a two-year period, of an intensive 'Tavistock' course. Perhaps, however, the most common experience will be a single visit to the child's home for the purpose of building up a more complete picture of the child than could be gained solely through visits to a pre-school group.

Frequently parents take pleasure in these student visits. In the home setting students do not usually seem like authority figures (as a health visitor would) and, as already mentioned, parents may positively welcome the chance to talk in detail about their child, but be sensible about what is discussed in the child's presence. They may take pride in the very fact that their child was specially chosen for this study. In practical terms, though, students should recognise that parents may have very little time to spare, especially if they are working long hours. Some parents may look to you for information about their child's activities at the pre-school group. If they do, it is wise to keep your replies to simple statements of fact. Try to concentrate on your own task of gathering information. Parents know their own child better than anyone else and you may discover interesting contrasts between *their* perceptions and those of the pre-school staff. Very occasionally parents refuse to have a student come to their home and this, of course, must be accepted. There may be a host of reasons for a refusal.

Where observations take place over a long period of time in the child's home (as in the 'Tavistock method'), their impact will doubtless be considerable. The parents will perhaps have to reorganise their schedule round the visits. They will also find that the presence of an outsider in the close intimate environment of the family home, however carefully the observer avoids direct participation in parent-child interactions, inevitably conditions their behaviour and responses. Indeed, home observations will almost certainly make parents more conscious of how they interact with their child and behave 'as parents'.

The impact on the individuals involved: the observer

Students in seminars tend to enjoy sharing experiences about their child observations. These experiences have usually been positive. The good humour in most pre-school groups is infectious and students sometimes re-tell certain episodes with amusement. Almost always someone has had to resist the temptation to join in.

During observations memories of childhood may be revived, often happy ones. On occasion, however, less comfortable, even disturbing reminders of the past may re-surface. 'It was,' one student remarked, 'the smell of plasticene which brought back the horrors of my school-days.' As an observer you may also come to realise the extent to which you are identifying with the child you are watching. In one instance a student was shocked at her partisanship in siding with 'her' child (i.e. the subject of her study) in a squabble over a tricycle. She found herself willing 'her' child to get the tricycle to the extent that, as she put it: 'I didn't care about the other kid'. Students who happen to be parents themselves may draw comparisons with their own children or, if their children are older, be reminded of their earlier years.

Your feelings about the observation you have carried out will inevitably be conditioned by many factors. Some of these will be personal – your situation in life, past experiences, education and culture. Others will stem from your theoretical standpoint and professional orientation (e.g. towards social work, education or health care), and others again from the circum-stances of the observation itself, including your choice of child. Your attitude may even be affected by your willingness to accept observation as a technique, especially in regard to children. Some people do have reservations about watching others in this deliberate way. You should remember, though, that the ultimate purpose of observation is to develop professional competence in work with children and families, and that planning for children's lives must be based on a proper foundation of understanding. From your own point of view, observation should help you to understand children and their range of behaviour better, to reassess your own preconceptions on the subject, and to practise watching intently and recording accurately. Finally you may well gain in self-confidence.

References and further reading

Drummond, M.J., Rouse, D. and Pugh, G. (1992) *Making Assessment Work*. London: National Children's Bureau.

Harrison, F. (1985) *A Father's Diary*. London: Fontana, Flamingo.

Irwin, D.M. and Bushnell, M.M. (1980) *Observational Strategies for Child Study*. New York: Holt Rinehart and Winston.

Miller, L., Rustin, M., Rustin, M. and Shuttleworth, J. (eds) (1989) *Closely Observed Infants*. London: Duckworth.

Sylva, K., Roy, C. and Painter, M. (1980) *Childwatching at Playgroup and Nursery School*. London: Grant McIntyre.

Photograph by Lucy Mortimer

Photograph by Rosemary Freeman

Photograph by Rosemary Freeman

Photograph by Jackie Baker

Photograph by Rosemary Freeman

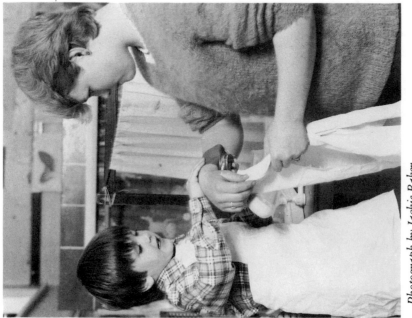

Photograph by Jackie Baker

Photograph by Sarah Cocke

CHAPTER FIVE

Child Observations
Exploring Themes

Introduction

Having collected data from a series of observational visits, what happens next? This chapter aims to introduce the reader to various ways of thinking about the gathered material. The possibilities are almost endless and what follows is a small selection of explorations. You might compare your gathered observations with fish caught in a net. The type and size of the net determines the type and size of the fish you catch, and Chapter Four of this book explains different techniques (or nets, to continue the analogy). Sometimes observational methods will have been used to investigate a particular problem or topic: for instance you may have been trying to discover how children attract the attention of adults and how you used the Time Sampling technique. On other occasions, observers will have been recording a small section of the daily life of a child, where the child's total behaviour is the subject. Using Naturalistic Observation or the Target Child method you will have collected several 'slices of life' of an individual child. Whichever techniques have been used you are now ready to examine and to analyse the records.

This chapter has been organised in themes. They are a sample from the many which might be explored. These particular themes have been selected because students on past courses have found them interesting and important, and also because they incorporate some recent developments in our thinking about children.

Observation is of course in the first place a tool, a method for collecting information. Beyond that it is an invaluable source of knowledge and understanding about children and their ecological context, and also has potential for changing the manner in which we think about what we see. Throughout this book readers are being encouraged to reflect on what is happening through the experience of observation. This chapter maintains this perspective.

Workers in all child-related professions appreciate the need to think broadly about children and their ecological context – the circumstances in which the next generation is growing up – and all can benefit from the experience of observation in the round. In addition, however, each profession will have its own agenda and will employ observational methods for the gathering of specific information. The purpose of this book is to offer guidance of a broader, more open-ended kind. For texts in more specialist areas, psychologists may use Pellegrini (1987) or Irwin and Bushnell (1980), psychotherapists may turn to Miller *et al.*, (1989), and teachers will draw on works appropriate to the children's age-group

Underlying principles of development

It is important to grasp certain fundamental characteristics of a child's development. The first has to do with the dramatic speed of growth, that is to say both physical and mental change, in the first five years. Picture in your mind's eye a new-born baby, a small sixteen-inch-long, wrapped-up bundle about eight pounds in weight. Certainly 'programmed' for rapid development, the infant just now seems very immature and fragile. Now picture a five-year-old in the school playground, organising the other children in a complicated imaginative game. Chattering and gesticulating she races across the play area and climbs nimbly up a climbing frame – already displaying considerable mobility and physical co-ordination, advanced skills in language, competence in the 'rules' of social relation-ships, and growing all-round confidence. Progress will never be so rapid again.

Another crucial feature of development is the drive (intrinsic motiva-tion) to explore, to find out, to master the environment. It is hard to understate the power of this force. We sometimes use the word 'curiosity' to describe it and call the behaviour we see, 'play'. A classic chapter by Jerome Bruner, 'The nature and uses of immaturity' (Bruner, 1976), highlights the value of a long period of 'playful' immaturity, which forms the basis of sophisticated behaviour in adulthood. Indeed, of all the animal kingdom, humans have the longest period of immaturity and vulnerability.

Human beings are also remarkable for their adaptability and flexibility. They have 'colonised' just about every environment on the planet. In part this adaptability is due to their direct learning ability, but they can also learn by proxy – in other words through others' experiences. They can be taught. They do not have to discover everything for themselves.

Furthermore, every child is unique and individual. The variety is astonishing and results from the differing combinations of genes and experiences, the constant interaction of the biological and the environmental. Parents regularly comment on the differences among their own offspring, perhaps not recognising that life experiences in the family can be altogether different, even though the genetic inheritance may be similar. Thus, the first-born is the sole focus of new parental attention, while the second-born enters an established family with parents who are no longer novices at the job. Because each child is unique, observers must avoid generalising about behaviour on the basis of a single child. Differences between children also stem in part from the cultural framework in which they grow up. Priorities and expectations will vary from society to society – to take an obvious example, the different attitudes to girls and boys. The child's environment is going to present opportunities and risks which, because children are both vulnerable and adaptable, will alter their lives (Garbarino, 1992).

Figure 5.1, while highlighting the chief features of development, is of course a drastic simplification of a dynamic process. Human beings are complex. There are many sides to our personalities, abilities and interests; most of us would strongly object to being thought of in only one dimension. In addition the different categories isolated in the diagram all interact in a way far more complicated than represented by the links shown. A 'holistic' view recognises this complexity. Even a cursory look at the diagram will suggest how the categories interact and how it may sometimes be problematic to locate an item of behaviour, noted during observation, in any one 'circle'. For instance some creative, aesthetic experiences (poems, songs, drama) will be speech-based, and thus overlap two categories. Similarly, a simple activity like a child dressing belongs with both 'Caring for Self' and 'Physical Skill Development'. Using this framework you can analyse your observational records and discover which categories are, and are not, represented. A framework emphasising the holistic view is preferable to the limited frameworks set out in many other textbooks.

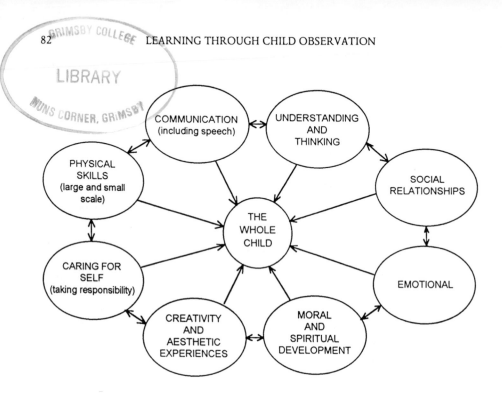

Figure 5.1. A holistic view of the developing child

Some practicalities

If you have been using the Naturalistic Observation or Target Child methods your first step will be to consider the child's behaviour and experience quite broadly. When you compare your observation with the diagram above you will recognise that your records do not cover all aspects of a child's progress. Some areas will be represented in more detail than others. Some areas may strike you as especially interesting. In that case you might choose a topic or area (for instance, imaginative play or language use), investigate your observations from that point of view, look at some literature and theories on the topic, and reflect on what you have seen. The Target Child method in particular facilitates the analysis of observations. Three possible topics for analysis would be – the length of concentration by the child on a theme, the types of task chosen by a child, or the sorts of social interaction the child has engaged in. Where appropriate some suggestions about possible ways of presenting data will be given, but this aspect is not over-emphasised because only small numbers of children and/or observations are involved.

The various themes identified below are far from exhaustive but will serve to illustrate the scope for analysis. The first group covers four specific aspects of development. The second group of themes includes play, special needs and 'settling in'.

Themes concerning development

1. Social development and cultural context

There is truth in the widespread belief of parents that children will learn *socially* from their pre-school group experiences and that this matters. A large and growing body of research examines this aspect of development and is reinforcing our understanding of the crucial importance of social relationships in personality growth.

One way of examining the nature of the social experiences that an observed child has engaged in can be found in Sylva *et al.*, (1980, p.137). If the grid for the Target Child method has been used you will find a column labelled *SOCIAL*. This is where you will now enter the social code for each minute of observation. By coding in this way you will be creating a summary of the child's social interaction or lack of it. The *social code* (derived from Sylva, 1980, pp.237–9) is simple to grasp:

SOL	Solitary
PAIR	Two people together (child plus another child)
SG	In a small group of three to five children
LG	In a large group of six or more children.
/P	'Parallel' – the child plays alone but close to another child or group

For instance PAIR/P means that the child plays near another child but quite independently. The children may be doing the same thing, but /P should be used unless they are interacting.

A circle drawn round PAIR, SG or LG indicates that an adult is involved. For instance PAIR means that the child is playing or chatting with an adult.

Having added the social codes to your observation, you can tally the amount of time spent in the various groupings. This information could be made into a bar graph, a Venn diagram or some other format which shows the proportions of time.

A very influential study (Parton, 1933) – though based on *one* nursery – suggests that children move through stages in their play as they grow older. Indeed it was this study that coined the phrase 'parallel play'. Parton's categories of play begin with the unoccupied child, and then (in order) the child as onlooker, and the child involved in solitary or independent play, in parallel activity, in associative play, and finally in co-operative play. There is a tendency for children to move through these stages but naturally they are an over-simplification. What may be more significant than the child's age is their newness in any particular group. It is also important to note the *quality* of the involvement with other people and the effect that adults may have on a child's activity. The involvement of an adult often increases the length of time a child sticks with a task. Adults can 'scaffold' the child's activity by providing suitable materials, perhaps by subdividing the task and making positive suggestions, but not taking over.

The second and third years of life show dramatic changes in a child's capacity to understand social rules. (This topic will be looked at again in the section below, *Development of understanding and thinking*.) Of course the rules and social conventions in a pre-school group may contrast, or even conflict, with those at home. Observers will notice that, in general, children seem to adapt to routines remarkably quickly, but there may be times when a child faces a confusing dilemma. Father says 'stand up and fight for yourself', in contradiction to the 'no-fighting' rule of the group. An Asian child is told not to make tea in a saucepan, when that is what she observes her mother doing every day.

The role and importance of the peer group in social development have tended to be ignored. This situation is now being rectified. In particular, Judy Dunn's observations of siblings in their families have produced some very revealing insights (Dunn, 1988 and 1993).

Social interactions for children in their pre-school years are not only about adapting to a group, learning how to share, and making friends. Children's cognitive development actually depends on social experiences. Learning, not just about the social but the factual world too, comes about through our interactions with other people, especially the members of our own cultural group. The work of Vygotsky (see Chapter Two) has strengthened our understanding of the process by which this probably happens. His view is that from the very moment of birth the child should be seen as a valued group member with whom experiences are shared. Children learn language, how to solve problems and about the environment, through these interactions. Vygotsky's famous phrase 'what a child can do with assistance to-day, she will be able to do by herself to-morrow' epitomises the nature of the learning process. The child is like an apprentice and the more competent members of the group (perhaps older children), 'scaffold' the child's learning experiences. Vygotsky insists that all learning is located in a cultural setting. (For further reading about this stimulating view see Meadows, 1993, or Miller, 1993.)

Finally a thought culled from Hazareesingh *et al.*, (1989) on cultural perspectives. Twentieth-century British society is very individualistic. We encourage children to be competitive rather than co-operative and we see childhood as separate from the adult world. Other cultures regard children very differently. Consider Hazareesingh's statement from Indian philosophy: 'the child should not be simply "brought up": there is an accompanying responsibility for the adult to enter into the child's mode of experiencing the world' (p.18).

2. Communication

Fluent communication through language by the age of five years is miraculous, and yet virtually everyone achieves this in whatever culture they grow up. So fascinating and puzzling is this skill that more has been written about language than about any other area of development. We use language for just about everything – to obtain what we want or need, to explain ourselves, to make friends, to solve problems, to entertain ourselves, to study and learn.

In your observations of eighteen-month-old infants to four-year-olds the talk you have been hearing comes from children in their most dramatic phase of language development. What might you be looking out for? A few suggestions are offered here – some topics being more concerned with the stages of development, and others with the circumstances which may encourage the acquisition of this vital tool.

You may first notice actual *speech production*. The clarity of the sounds, perhaps certain mispronunciations or even omissions of parts of words, may strike you as interesting. Whether this is just a normal stage in speech growth, a problem relating to the production of speech sounds, or an indication of some other difficulty (such as hearing loss) could be a topic for investigation. Sheridan (1973) provides a list of speech characteristics in age-related order which may give you an indication of what might be expected.

Next to the mechanics of sound production, a subject of considerable fascination is the child's use of *grammar*. Steven Pinker's *The Language*

Instinct (1994), a current best-seller, is strongly recommended for its account of how humans learn to use language. Pinker, drawing on the work of Noam Chomsky, claims that language is innate – that every human being is born not only with a special capacity to acquire language, but with a faculty for grammar. Language can be compared with walking, in that all children will learn it without being taught. In your observations you may want to examine carefully the kinds of grammatical structures the child is using. They will probably be beyond the single-word stage and likely to be past telegraphic speech (where just key words are used, such as: where Mummy gone?). You may well find some examples of over-extended or over-generalised rules, as in 'She goed to her Mum', where the child applies the normal rule for forming the past tense to what happens to be an irregular verb. What is remarkable at this stage is how much children get right. Pinker points out that in order to use the suffix -s properly you have to understand four sorts of distinction:

1.   I walk but he walks ('first person' versus 'third person')

2.   He walks but they walk (singular versus plural)

3.   He walks but he walked (present tense versus past tense)

4.   He walks to school, but he is walking to school (simple present versus continuous present).

It seems confusing, but more than ninety per cent of three-and-a-half year-olds used the correct form in the study reported by Pinker (1994, p.44).

Another topic you might consider is *language style and purposes*. How are children using language at this phase of their development? Do they talk about the here and now or the past? How do they join in conversations? A good chapter on this subject is 'Conversations with the pre-school child' in Wood *et al.* (1980).

Closely associated with the styles of language used are the *situations which encourage conversation*. Should you wish to study this you will find ideas in *Working with Under Fives*, by Wood *et al.*, the book just referred to. Do children talk much to other children?. Do they talk more when they are in large or small groups? What kinds of tasks give opportunities for conversation? Do they talk much to other children? Gordon Wells' research based on recordings made in children's own homes (1987) found that the circumstances which correlated with 'good' language development involved the presence of attentive, sensitive adults who followed and supported their children's own efforts and attempts to solve problems. Further, the telling and reading of stories at the pre-school stage was associated with the achievement of reading skills at the age of seven. Edward Melhuish, in his investigations into the quality of pre-school experiences (1990), examined differences in interactional experience. He recorded various dimensions including the amount of talk initiated by adults and directed towards the child, the reverse of this (that is, child talk to the adult), and talk between children. He concluded that the nature of the interactions between adults and children is a key indicator of quality.

As an observer in both the home and the pre-school setting you may be able to compare the communication patterns in these two environments. Tizard and Hughes researched this aspect, though observing girls only (1984). They found striking differences, and, to the dismay of some nursery teachers, the language used in the nursery school was far less complex. The cultural differences between any home and the pre-school group, and the resulting differences in language use, can be very great. With bilingual children this contrast will be even more significant. Children may also be at quite different levels in the various languages of their immediate environment. Some children may in fact be multilingual. In some Pakistani families Panjabi would be the mother tongue, Urdu the formal language and Arabic the language used in religion (Siraj-Blatch-ford, 1994). In the pre-school group you might compare the child's use of language while occupied in different activities – for instance playing in the home corner as compared to playing with standardised toys such as jigsaw puzzles. Does the bilingual child use her/his own home language at all in the pre-school? Other topics for reflection concerning the environment and the bilingual child – and hence encouragement to use the mother tongue – include the availability of bilingual books, the nature of other equipment (such as the contents of the home corner) and adults in the group who are themselves bilingual.

3. Attachment and children's understanding of emotions

A human infant could not live long without adult help. Babies and young children require food, shelter, protection, love and care of every kind. For sheer survival they simply must have ways of engaging – and retaining – adult attention. They have to be in close proximity to the adults they so much depend on and who know how to pick up their signals and respond to their individual needs. The 'attachment' that develops between parents (or whoever stands in for the parents) and infants has been briefly described above in Chapter Two, and indeed from an evolutionary point of view attachment behaviour makes real sense.

You may observe young children displaying attachment behaviour, and keeping contact in various ways, according to their age, personality, the cultural setting, and so on. They may, for example, 'cling', or cry to attract attention, smile inappropriately, talk incessantly, and refuse to let the adult out of sight. Children who have grown confident in their family settings will, by the age of three, usually be able to play independently without constant reassurance and recognition from the 'attachment figure'. In day care settings, however, the 'key-worker system' (where each child has a care worker specifically allocated) recognises that small children need continuity and individualised attention. Goldschmied and Jackson (1994) explain how this might work in practice.

Attachment is a much-researched and debated topic (for summaries see Lamb, 1985; or Rutter, 1991) but it cannot be denied that *all* humans need affectionate and reliable relationships, certainly in childhood, and probably throughout their lives.

Through all their early experiences of people, in or outside family, children are learning to understand emotions. Paul Harris has been examining the processes by which this happens. In his article 'The child's understanding of emotion' (1994) he summarises research on children who have experienced two types of distorted or extreme emotional environments – one in which the person primarily responsible for looking after the child was suffering from chronic depression, the other charac-terised by angry family rows (perhaps as the family splits up). Depressed adults can blight children's experiences through their high level of irritability, their unenthusiastic reactions, their failure to respond and show interest. This may set up a behaviour pattern so that when these children meet with novel experiences in the future, even away from the depressed adults, they may be resistant or unwilling to respond. Aggressive environ-ments can have an equally negative effect and result in other patterns of behaviour. To protect themselves the children sometimes learn to become very still and intensely watchful, seeming almost frozen, or else smile excessively as if continuing to placate the violent actors in scenes of domestic violence (even if they themselves were not the target). You may observe behaviours such as these in group settings.

While it is interesting to note the methods by which children reveal their emotions, and the language they use to describe how they feel, it is also fascinating to examine how they interpret and talk about other people's feelings. The extent to which families both show and talk about their emotions varies enormously. Some children will therefore have acquired an extensive vocabulary and be able to describe feelings and meanings, while others will not.

4. The development of understanding and thinking

Everyday words have been used for the title of this section – that is, understanding and thinking. In other textbooks you would be likely to find the terms 'cognitive' development (or in older books, 'intellectual' development). The word 'understanding' suggests comprehension and knowledge, as well as a sympathetic awareness of others. Thinking, on the other hand, implies a more conscious process of reasoning and problem-solving. However, the two concepts are closely linked and when you analyse your studies of pre-school children you will find evidence of both. Often they will be revealed through the language children use as they report on past events, using their memories. It will also be evident in their imaginative play with other children, in their negotiating with their peers. Sometimes it will be shown through actions, not words, as when they put farm animals together or match colours, in other words displaying the ability to classify through their knowledge about similarity and difference. It is likely that you will pick out other logical or mathematical knowledge, such as putting things in order of size (serialisation) or using counting words. You will observe children trying to solve problems; say, how to construct a model from old cardboard boxes or toy bricks. As they gradually take more personal responsibilty, showing their independence and initiative (for example in organising their own, and other children's, play) you are seeing yet more evidence through words and actions of what we may now term cognitive development.

Two aspects of the developing mind have recently received considerable research attention and both give possible explanations of certain kinds of behaviour which we observe in young children. Both derive from Piaget's work. The first involves children's understanding of their environment (the physical world around them). The second is more about their understanding of how other people think. A little background on Piaget's theory is necessary here. As already mentioned in Chapter Two Piaget was trying to explain how children come to make knowledge their own, how they construct concepts in their minds. Through observations of children, especially his own, he came to believe that the processes by which they make sense of the world change by definite stages as they grow older. These stages of development are described in many books (for example Meadows, 1993, or Sylva and Lunt, 1980) and you may wish to consult one of these. The children you observe will probably be at the second major stage, one which Piaget called *pre-operational* (covering roughly the years from two to seven). Before that, children will have been passing through the *sensori-motor* period, when learning is based on exploring the world through the senses, when discoveries about the properties of objects are made by touching and grasping them, dropping or shaking them, or banging them together (and in earlier months, putting objects in the mouth). However, at the next, *pre-operational* stage (so-called because the child has not yet reached the *concrete operations* stage, when they have much firmer and more logical beliefs about phenomena) Piaget describes children's behaviour as 'egocentric'. This does not mean simple selfishness. The theory is rather that children at this stage still tend to interpret the world in terms of themselves, because they have not yet completely differentiated their own persons from other people and objects. At this stage, too, children typically focus on the more obvious visual features of objects or events, ignoring other evidence. An example of this would be their claim that a lump of playdough or plasticene amounts to more when rolled into a long, thin shape than when the same lump is made into a ball. Children before the age of seven are also likely to explain natural phenomena in terms of human actions. (For some criticisms of Piaget's ideas see Chapter Two. Otherwise, for a detailed and readable discussion, Margaret Donaldson's *Children's Minds* (1978) is highly recommended.)

Following on from Piaget, Chris Athey (1990) has made a study of the way children build up their mental *schemata* (structures in the mind). Her interest has centred on the very basic concepts such as movement, enclosure and shape. She explains that in order to grasp any concept fully children will engage in many varied and, in a way, repetitive activities. Thus, a child who is coming to terms with the 'enclosure' schema (which includes a cluster of ideas such as 'containing', 'enveloping', 'surrounding') will be observed selecting tasks which relate thematically to this schema. The child may build houses with bricks, draw circular shapes, climb inside big boxes whenever there is a chance, fill and empty containers at the water trough – in other words choose activities and equipment which give opportunities to 'work' on the schema. Athey believes that engagement in the process provides motivation, an insatiable desire to try out the schema in action, play, talk, paint or whatever.

The second theory currently of great interest concerns what Rutter (1992) calls 'everyday mind-reading' and which others describe as a 'theory of mind'. Somehow children develop an idea of how minds work. How do they come to do this and to conceive what is going on in other people's heads? When do they realise that other people can have different thoughts from their own? At what age are they likely to recognise that people may say or do one thing but mean another, as they do in jokes or deception? (A very simplified account of the probable phases of understanding is given here but for further reading you might look at Astington *et al.*, (1988) or Wellman (1990).)

Even around the age of six months babies demonstrate that they know that other people can actually think about what is of interest to them (as babies) when they point to a teddy bear, look at the adult, and then at the teddy bear again in the expectation that the adult will take notice. Trevarthen (1980) has called this intersubjectivity: 'I know that you know what I am thinking about'. At around two years pretending games are common. The child picks up a banana, holds it to her ear and talks into it, as if it were a telephone. Before children are three years old they are using words such as *know, think, remember*, and can apply them to other people. Three-year-olds can distinguish between real and purely mental ideas. Supposing they are told that one child *has* a biscuit and that another child is *thinking* about a biscuit, they can tell you which biscuit can be eaten. On the other hand three-year-olds have difficulty with the 'false-belief task'. This can be shown by telling them a story about a girl who puts a sweet in a basket and then goes out of the room. While she is away another child comes in, takes the sweet out of the basket and places it instead in a box. The researcher then asks 'Where will the little girl look for the sweet when she comes back?' Three-year-old children usually say 'In the box'. They fail to appreciate that the little girl could not know what had happened. Around four, however, children do begin to understand. They have become much more aware of other people's beliefs, intentions and wishes. They are beginning to distinguish between the real and the imaginary. Most children develop this vital insight into other people's motives. Without this personal 'theory of mind' not only will relationships become very difficult, but the child (or older person too) risks being deceived and manipulated. People with Autism or Asperger Syndrome (a milder form of Autism) lack this understanding of other people's intentions. It is not a question of not feeling empathy for others but of an inability to perceive and interpret all the meanings which other people are communicating.

When you examine your observations you may find instances of children telling jokes, or lies, misunderstanding each other, playing imaginatively with each other, and so on. All these occasions afford insights into the way that children comprehend (or fail to comprehend) other people's meaning.

A sample of other themes

1. Settling in

When a child joins a pre-school group for the first time what kinds of behaviour might be seen? There will of course be differences depending on the child's age, whether a brother or sister has been a member, and whether the newcomer already has friends or acquaintances in the group. The policy of the group on settling children in is also highly significant in making the transition from home to group an easy one. It is common to arrange a series of accompanied preliminary visits by the child and parent before the proper starting date. These allow the child to become used to the place, the people and the activities on offer. Parents may also stay for a few sessions, or part of sessions, to help their child adjust comfortably. Yet even with all these helpful opportunities the experience of joining a big group, perhaps of twenty-four children, can be stressful. Some children may have come from quiet, fairly solitary backgrounds. Until now they may have encountered relatively few children, and those who have been with a child minder may have had only a small group to play with. Settling in may also be more difficult for children who have recently had major changes in their lives. A child who has been hospitalised, for instance, or suffered a family break-up, a house move, or even the birth of a new sibling, might find adjustment extra hard.

It is not too difficult to empathise with the child new to pre-school, and to recall our own feelings as an adult coming into a group of strangers. We are likely to behave in ways very similar to children. Five reactions are characteristic. The first is watchfulness. The newcomer is likely to spend a great deal of time simply looking around at what is going on. The 'new' child will be observing the other children, picking up clues about what to do, where to go, what is allowed, and so on. Besides the many people that have to be made sense of, there are also all the activities. The leaders will have tried to make the play seem enticing, but the newcomer may still be unsure what it is all about. Watching those who are familiar with the materials may seem to be the safest bet. Hence the newcomer almost always keeps rather still. This stillness, the second type of reaction you may observe, is associated with the watching, for you can only keep a careful watch if you remain reasonably stationary. I have spotted children just sitting on a chair at one side of the room for as much as an hour, simply 'taking it all in'. If you have used the Target Child method, the code SA/AWG (standing around, aimless wander or gaze, see Appendix) will categorise this form of behaviour. In contrast, some new children exhibit a third behaviour pattern. They go to the other extreme and flit like a butterfly around the room, perhaps handling a few objects as they go, but avoiding involvement in anything. The code for this is RO (roaming). Drawing a simple plan of the layout of the play room would allow you to map the child's movements in such a case. Studying this can reveal the extent of 'roaming' behaviour.

The fourth type of symptomatic behaviour is the reluctance to engage in talk or conversation. The Target Child Language Record column may remain almost blank. Once again, empathising may help to make sense of your observations. Adults in unfamiliar situations tend to 'play safe' and often do more listening than talking.

The final way in which children reveal their uncertainties about a strange pre-school situation is by anxiety traits. Familiar examples of such traits include fiddling with hair or clothes, thumb-sucking, cuddling a soft toy or clinging to a reminder from home (a bit of blanket perhaps).

McGrew, in his classic study (1972), picked out four of these modes of behaviour, just watching, lack of activity, little talk and use of a comforter. To this group I have added roaming or 'butterfly-like' flitting.

As a topic for a case study, the adaptation of a child into a new environment observing over a few months has much to recommend it. You are likely to observe changes in the areas described above. You may also notice how friendships with individual children develop, how particular kinds of adult support help to establish the child as a participating member of the group, and how certain activities seem to be effective in easing the child into this new life. Comparing the child's use of language over a period (say, from the first week to two months later) can be equally instructive. You may find out how much that child talks to adults as opposed to children, or whether they talk mainly to one person. You could examine what kinds of conversations are engaged in and how language is used (on this see Wood *et al.*, 1980). The adjustments that some children have to make, especially children newly arrived in this country (possibly as refugees), are potentially enormous. In this respect it is worth pointing out that the Children Act requires pre-school groups to take proper account of the cultural origins of every child, though there are still uncertainties about putting this regulation into practice. (Helpful guidance here will be found in Brown, 1993; Hazareesingh *et al.*, 1989; and Siraj-Blatchford, 1994.)

2. Imaginative play

Most of the activity you have observed you will probably term 'play'. Other ways in which children have been spending their time, such as listening to a story or carrying out directed tasks, toileting or tidying up, are clearly not play. What then characterises play? Probably everyone would agree that it is an enjoyable activity, intrinsically motivated, usually open-ended (in not having a particular goal), not obligatory, and often, though not always, 'non-literal' (Garvey, 1977). This last characteristic refers to *pretend* or *imaginative* play, where a person or object is thought of 'as if' it were someone or something else: 'I'll be Batman, this curtain is my cloak'. Children also engage in another type of play which is not pretend or imaginative (or ludic as it is sometimes called). In *exploratory* play children are trying to find out the properties of materials, how objects work, what happens when you do things to them. So you may observe children with playdough (perhaps experiencing it for the first time) pummelling it, poking it, flattening it, rolling it and so on. You could regard such activity as a kind of scientific investigation. When given something new, children inevitably explore in this way before embarking on imaginative play.

But this section will largely concentrate on imaginative play and some of the ways in which you might analyse your observations. First of all you might consider what types of imaginative play you have recorded. Were the children playing with miniature, but real-world objects, such as toy cars, or home-corner objects such as saucepans. In other words, were they imitating real behaviour they have observed or, alternatively, were they creating fresh realities, pretending that the dough is a bird's nest, and the space behind the couch a cave? Clearly the equipment made available in the pre-school group will influence the likelihood of which form of play the children might select.

Reflections on this topic should lead you to examine the situations most likely to give rise to imaginative play. Does play with dressing-up clothes and the home-corner involve more imaginative play than construction with large wooden bricks, planks and boxes? What about painting and drawing, are children engaged imaginatively here? What do they say about their pictures? If you have used the Target Child method and coded the different types of *task* (see Appendix) you will be able to see how much time 'your' child has been spending at any particular one, whether music or 'large muscle movement' (e.g. running or climbing) or whatever.

The Target Child method will also give you information about the social setting for that period of play, in other words who the child was with. (You can of course extract all this information from Naturalistic observation too.) Imaginative play with another child or children is called socio-dramatic play, as distinct from solitary or parallel play. When playing with others, children are challenged to use language to explain what is going happen: 'I'll be the Mummy, you be the baby'. They may have to persuade their friend(s) that the game is worth playing: 'If you are the baby you can lie in the bed with the nice covers.' Sequences of this kind involve problem-solving and creativity as well as 'everyday mind-reading'.

It may also be worth looking at how a theme is carried through various tasks and situations, whether in solitary imaginative play or collaborative, socio-dramatic play. Two children were looking at a book about a picnic together. 'Why don't we have a picnic?' From the home corner they gathered plastic mugs and plates and stuffed them into bags. They found papers and pencils and 'wrote' letters of invitation to friends. Having encouraged these further children to join in, they set off for the climbing frame which they took over for the picnic. This whole episode lasted about half-an-hour and illustrates the fact that some small children (a three-year-old and a three-and-a-half-year-old) can maintain concentration on a topic for a considerable period of time. The length of time children stay with an activity is in fact another topic worthy of study (see Sylva *et al.*, 1980). What kinds of play activity do engage children's attention for long periods?

Kathy Sylva and her colleagues examined the quality of play, using the words 'simple' and 'complex'. They were investigating different pre-school activities to find out which ones enhanced children's play, and made it more challenging, so causing the children to persevere, create something, work towards a goal and be truly involved. They divided activity into complex (high cognitive challenge) and simple (ordinary cognitive challenge). Complex activity was 'novel, creative, imaginative, productive', whereas simple activity was 'familiar routine, stereotyped, repetitive, unproductive' (p.60). (The whole chapter on complex and simple play is decidedly thought-provoking.)

The debate, amongst psychologists especially, about the value of play (Smith, 1988) and the frequent juxtaposition of 'play' with 'work' may suggest scepticism about the benefits of play. However Furth and Kane (1992) have drawn attention to a range of interpretations of the concept of 'play'. Some authors (Bruner, Vygotsky, Sylva) have stressed the contribution of play to cognitive development, while others, like Rubin (1980), emphasise the social skills which can be learned through play. Catherine Garvey (1977) moreover points out that language development is enhanced through play, while yet another group of authors emphasise psychodynamic aspects. Freud's influence remains strong here, but some recent researchers (e.g. Fein, 1989) and therapists claim that play is beneficial in dealing with anxious and unhappy children. There is yet another opinion, that play needs no special justification: it is valuable for itself as well as giving an opportunity for cultural creativity. (Furth and Kane (1992) give a lovely account of their observations of 'Going to a ball'.)

All children in their early years, in whatever culture they live, will play, but just how adults regard this activity does differ among societies and at different times in history. When economic or basic survival needs are high on the agenda, children's playful activity is likely to be given lower value.

3. Gender differences in pre-school

Interest in the differing characteristics of females and males is pretty well universal. Observations of children regularly provoke discussions based on comparisons of girls and boys in their choice of toys, their types of play, and their general behaviour. The debate then focuses on the relative contributions of biological inheritance and social environment. We can state categorically that social conditioning begins even before the moment of birth. Parents of new-borns have been found to refer to boy babies as 'big' and 'strong' whereas girls were talked of as 'pretty' (in this research, difference in weight was controlled for). Boy babies were also immediately thought of in the long term, with speculations about such future possibilities as carrying on the father's business (Cole and Cole, 1993).

The subtle and diverse influences leading to a child's concept of gender role and consequent behaviour patterns are everywhere – in the media, the packaging of toys and foods, the social contacts with children of the same age group, and the role models within the immediate neighbourhood or family. We know that children become aware of the concept of gender from a very early age. Between twelve and twenty-four months children show that they realise the gender difference between their mother and father and between boys and girls. They use the correct labels, girl, boy, woman, man, she, he, from two years onwards. From three to five years they achieve greater stability of the concept, aware that they themselves will remain the same gender throughout their lives. Finally they come to understand the notion of constancy, that while outward appearances may change, the gender of a person remains constant.

The sophistication of children's awareness of their social environment, and of gender roles, before they start school, has come to be recognised only in the last fifteen years or so. Children observe and absorb the adult world, but it would be wrong to assume that it is all a one-way process, of adults conditioning children. Barrie Thorne (1993) from her extensive observations found that children affect each other, actively constructing their own reality; they were not restricted to learning from adults (p.3).

Choice of playthings may seem to be a simple indicator of the child's stereotyped gender-role but that can be misleading. Certainly you may well observe more boys than girls playing with large wooden bricks, and vice versa with dolls, but in their review of research Chris Henshall and Jacqueline McGuire (1986) make three points which should help observers guard against over-generalising. First, the environment, nature and ethos of the pre-school group affect the pattern of toy use. Next they claim 'children actually spend most of their time playing with toys which are not gender-differentiated' (p.139), although against this it may be argued that children do seem to view many toys or activities as more appropriate for boys or for girls. Their third conclusion is that gender *differences* are not necessarily gender *preferences*. If boys did play with building blocks more than girls, girls nonetheless played with building blocks three times as much as with dolls. Your observations during pre-school sessions will inevitably be brief and limited, and as a result you will not be in a position to generalise very much from them. All the same the relative use of toys by the two gender groups is worth thinking about.

The setting or context of the different play areas and the adults' behaviour in relation to these may be very significant. Consider for instance the typical use of outdoor play equipment (wheeled toys, climbing frames, etc.) in British pre-schools. This area of play is often seen as giving children a chance to 'let off steam' with the adult adopting a custodial role – in other words just ensuring that no one is at risk of injury, but otherwise keeping out of the action. Since boys are more likely to choose to play outside, they may therefore experience less constructive and creative adult input in their play. It is not simply a matter of the boys' own preference, for boys (even from the age of two) are generally allowed, even encouraged, to play on more dangerous outdoor apparatus. Incidentally they also receive much less comfort than girls should they hurt themselves (Henshall and McGuire, 1986, p.160). Not surprisingly boys have higher accident rates at all ages than girls. Boys, however, are likely to get very much more attention overall than girls. In one typical study of a class of four-year-olds the teacher spent sixty per cent of her time with the boys and forty per cent with the girls (Ebbeck, 1985). Further discussion of this topic will be found in Croll and Moses (1991).

Studies of whether boys play in a more aggressive manner than girls suggest that there is indeed a gender difference. However, the various research procedures (observations and sampling techniques) are not easy to compare and there are problems over definitions. What counts as 'aggressive behaviour', for example? Sometimes verbal insults are included on the checklist, sometimes not. Even rough-and-tumble play may be labelled 'aggressive behaviour'. In some cases boys have been found dominating certain play areas, for example the climbing frame, making it very difficult for girls even to play there (Skelton, 1991).

Gender differences in pre-school settings from another angle have been reported in Sara Häggland's article about Swedish observations (1993). She was trying to determine the effect of pre-school group experience on the development of what may be called 'prosocial competence'. Prosocial behaviour includes empathy, recognising other people's needs, and acting helpfully. Helpfulness of a caring, nurturing kind tends to be associated with the female role, although help in situations involving risk and bravery has male associations. In general Häggland discovered that prosocial behaviour was almost exclusively confined to free-play activities and took the form of older children helping younger ones. As to gender issues, girls were more likely to see themselves collaborating *with* the adults in helping other children, while boys proposed that *either* they *or* the adult would help. The consequences of the almost entirely female staffing of pre-school groups may be more significant than we know. (For further reading about prosocial behaviour see Eisenberg and Mussen, 1989.)

A final characteristic that you might observe is the choice of same-sex play partners. From around the age of three or four children most often show a preference for play with members of their own sex. Nonetheless, staff are advised to find ways of encouraging mixed groupings, for boys and girls to listen to and value each other (Skelton, 1991). (For further reading about children's friendships see Rubin, 1980.)

Adult awareness of sexism at the pre-school stage is growing, but girls continue to be treated more gently and are less expected to assert themselves, while boys will be told not to cry, not to show their feelings. (Information about sexism and other forms of discrimination will be found in Dixon, 1989, which studies children's playthings, and in Brown, 1993, a short practical guide.)

4. Special needs

The term 'need' requires careful handling. Its usage has been subjected to fine scrutiny by Woodhead (1991) who reminds us that the word carries varied meanings, some having universal validity but others only relative to certain cultural and social settings. The more particular phrase 'special needs' has been widely used since the publication of the Warnock Report (DES, 1987), but with the advent of the Children Act (1989) and its somewhat different definition of 'need', the terminology has become confusing for parents, students and anyone else not engaged daily in the field. The Warnock Report attempted to move away from the notion of 'handicapped' children, to broaden the way in which disability is conceptualised, suggesting that many children would at some time need special help (possibly up to 20%). Children with special needs were, as far as possible, to be integrated into normal provision, though their individual requirements should be properly assessed and a *statement* made of what would be required for that child. Local authorities in fact remain bound by law to make such statements for children between the ages of two and nineteen. The 1989 Children Act, however, has a different approach. A child is deemed to be 'in need' if there are doubts whether she/he will achieve a reasonable standard of health and all-round development (see Section 17 [10]). A child is considered 'disabled' if blind, deaf or dumb, suffering from a mental disorder, or physically handicapped (Section

17[11]). Not surprisingly the Children Act has been criticised for the revival of the label of disability and in particular the stigmatising term 'deaf and dumb'.

Students initially learning the skills of observation and general development will have more than enough in terms of new ideas to work on. For this reason it may be better to study *any* child rather than specifically to seek out one identified as having 'special educational needs' (on the Warnock definition) or 'in need' (according to the Children Act). But if you are observing a child with special needs this provides an opportunity to view the child's experience 'in the round', and not just to focus on the disability.

In the course of your observation, however, you may identify some behaviour which you suspect warrants concern. For instance students have sometimes noticed, after several observations, that the child assumed to be just rather quiet is very withdrawn, or that the language record reveals serious strains in the child's family life, or that the child seems not to hear well. Because you are observing a child in perhaps her/his first group experience, some of these problems may be showing up for the first time. Should you discover anything which seems amiss, your responsibility is to talk to the leader of the group, bearing in mind of course that as an inexperienced observer you might easily be mistaken.

Early identification of any impairment, disability, adjustment problem, or risk to development is of the utmost importance. Treatment or some form of intervention at the pre-school stage is preferable to delaying action until later and may actually prevent secondary problems arising.

Most pre-schools are very welcoming to children with disabilities and to their parents, recognising the rights of all children to equality of opportunity. The ways in which every child, disabled or not, benefits from the facilities available (perhaps through adaptations and innovations and special projects) should be noted. In the end, however, inadequate access and facilities may still preclude the full involvement of some children.

Your observations may reveal stereotyping and the use of negative language towards people with disabilities. Children may misunderstand, or even seem to fear, some types of impairment in others. The responsibility is with adults to give children accurate information, to talk openly about the matter and to create a positive atmosphere for the whole group.

5. Children seeking adult attention

This section will look at how to deal with a specific type of observation record – Time Sampling – based on the topic of children seeking adult attention. Chapter Four set out the method and gave details about the preparatory stages. The purpose of Time Sampling is to discover the frequency of whatever aspect of behaviour is being targeted. First the focus must be clearly defined: in this case a child who seems to be making very heavy demands on the adults. The second is the preparation of a checklist of the categories of behaviour to be noted – in this example acceptable/ undesirable forms of verbal/non-verbal attention-seeking. The frequency of recording times must also be chosen – say, every minute for thirty minutes. After the observation comes the analysis of the observational record. The ticks for each type of behaviour are counted up, thus revealing the frequency of each type. In order to compare the four categories you could draw a bar chart like this:

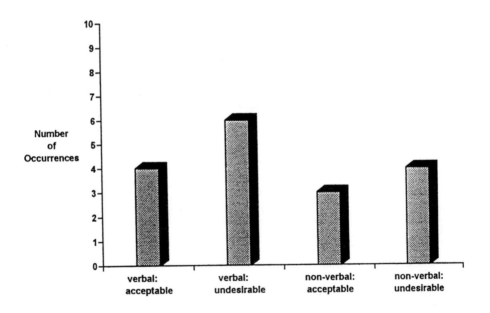

Figure 5.2. Totals of attention-seeking behaviour, 10.00–10.30am

From the chart you can see the relative occurrences of the chosen behaviour patterns over a specified period of time. This more objective statistical information sometimes serves to alter earlier perceptions of the child's interactions with adults.

At this stage other questions might be asked. Has the selected period of time yielded a representative sample of the target behaviour? If you are in doubt you may decide to repeat the observation at some other half-hour period, perhaps towards the end of the session. A further option would be to observe on another day of the week. Sometimes behaviour on Monday mornings (following the week-end) is rather different from later in the week.

Once you have acquired your data through Time Sampling and analysed it, you should reflect on what the information tells you. You may be surprised to find that your first impressions were ill-judged. For instance, it is easy to be misled by flamboyant, noisy behaviour and perhaps become somewhat irritated by it. On closer examination of your sample, it may become obvious that though the child is very 'noticeable' the tactics used to attract adult attention are generally acceptable and not a cause for real concern.

On the other hand a child might seem desperate for adult attention, using virtually any ploy, possibly interfering with other children's play. You may wonder whether this child has had poor 'attachment' experiences (see the earlier section in this chapter on *Attachment and children's under-standing of emotions*). Nevertheless, whatever the underlying reason, if the child behaves in a way which interferes with normal activities in the pre-school group (and which might lead to problems at the school stage) then assessments will need to be made as to whether any or what type of intervention is appropriate.

References and further reading

Astington, J.W., Harris, P.L. and Olson, D.R. (1988) *Developing Theories of Mind.* Cambridge: Cambridge University Press.

Athey, C. (1990) *Extending Thought in Young Children.* London: Paul Chapman.

Brown, B. (1993) *All our Children.* London: BBC.

Bruner, B., Jolly, A. and Sylva, K. (1976) *Play: Its Role in Development and Evolution.* Harmondsworth: Penguin.

Cole, M. and Cole. S. (1993) *The Development of Children.* 2nd edition. New York: Scientific American Books.

Croll, P. and Moses, D. (1991) 'Sex roles in the primary classroom.' In M. Woodhead *et al. Growing up in a Changing Society.* London: Routledge.

Department of Education and Science (1978) *Report of the Committee of Inquiry into the Education of Handicapped Children and Young People (Warnock Report)*. London: HMSO.

Dixon, B. (1989) *Playing Them False: A Study of Children's Toys, Games and Puzzles*. Stoke-on Trent: Trentham Books.

Donaldson, M. (1978) *Children's Minds*. London: Croom Helm.

Dunn, J. (1988) *The Beginnings of Social Understanding*. Oxford: Basil Blackwell.

Dunn, J. (1993) *Young Children's Close Relationships: Beyond Attachment*. London: Sage Publications.

Ebbeck, M. (1985) 'Teachers' behaviour towards boys and girls.' An *OMEP (UK) Update*. World Organisation for Early Childhood Education.

Eisenberg, N. and Mussen, P. (1989) *The Roots of Prosocial Behaviour in Children*. Cambridge: Cambridge University Press.

Fein, G.G. (1989) 'Mind, meaning and affect: Proposals for a theory of pretense.' *Developmental Review 9*, 344–363.

Furth, H.G. and Kane, S.R. (1992) 'Children constructing society: A new perspective on children at play.' In H. McGurk (ed) *Childhood Social Development: Contemporary Perspectives*. Hove, Sussex: Lawrence Erlbaum.

Garbarino, J. (1992) *Children and Families in the Social Environment*. 2nd Edition. Berlin: De Gruyter.

Garvey, C. (1977) *Play*. London: Fontana/Open.

Goldschmied, E. and Jackson, S. (1994) *People Under Three: Young Children in Day Care*. London: Routledge.

Hägglund, S. (1993) 'Gender and prosocial competence.' In *European Early Childhood Education Research Association Journal 1*, 2, 67–80.

Harris, P.L. (1994) 'Children's understanding of emotion: Developmental change and the family environment.' *Journal of Child Psychology and Psychiatry 35*, 1, 3–28.

Harris, P.L. (1989) *Children and Emotion*. Oxford: Basil Blackwell.

Hazareesingh, S,. Sims, K. and Anderson, P. (1989) *Educating the Whole Child*. London: Building Blocks.

Henshall, C. and McGuire, J. (1986) In M. Richards and P. Light (eds) *Children of Social Worlds*. Oxford: Basil Blackwell.

Her Majesty's Stationery Office (1989) *Children Act*. London: HMSO.

Irwin, M. and Bushnell, M. (1980) *Observational Strategies for Child Study*. New York: Holt, Rinehart and Winston.

Lamb, M. (ed) (1985) *Infant–Mother Attachment*. Hillsdale, New Jersey: Laurence Erlbaum Associates.

Lindon, J. (1993) *Child Development from Birth to Eight*. London: National Children's Bureau.

McGrew, W.C. (1972) *An Ethological Study of Children's Behaviour*. New York and London: Academic Press.

Meadows, S. (1993) *The Child as Thinker: The Development and Acquisition of Cognition in Childhood*. London: Routledge.

Melhuish, E. (1990) 'Types of child care at 18 months – 1. Differences in interactional experience.' *Journal of Child Psychology and Psychiatry 31*, 6, 849–859.

Miller, L., Rustin, M., Rustin, M. and Shuttleworth, J. (1989) *Closely Observed Infants*. London: Duckworth.

Miller, P.H. (1993) *Theories of Developmental Psychology*. New York: W.H. Freeman and Co.

Moyles, J.R. (ed) (1994) *The Excellence of Play*. Milton Keynes: Open University Press.

Parton, M.B. (1933) 'Social participation among pre-school children.' *Journal of Abnormal and Social Psychology 27*, 243–269.

Pellegrini, A.D. (1987) *Applied Child Study: A Developmental Approach*. Hillsdale, NJ: Lawrence Erlbaum Associates.

Pinker, S. (1994) *The Language Instinct*. Harmonsdworth: Penguin.

Rubin, K. (1980) *Children's Play*. San Francisco: Jossey Bass.

Rutter, M. (1991) 'A fresh look at "maternal deprivation".' In P. Bateson (ed) *The development and Integration of Behaviour: Essays in Honour of Robert Hinde*. Cambridge: Cambridge University Press.

Rutter, M. (1992) *Developing Minds: Challenge and Continuity across the Lifespan*. Harmondsworth: Penguin.

Sheridan, M. (1973) *Children's Developmental Progress from Birth to Five: The Stycar Sequences*. London: NFER.

Siraj-Blatchford, I. (1994) *The Early Years: Laying the Foundation for Racial Equality*. Stoke-on-Trent: Trentham Books.

Skelton, C. (1991) 'Demolishing "The house that Jack built".' In M. Woodhead *et al. Growing up in a Changing Society*. London: Routledge.

Smith, P.K. (1988) 'Children's play and its role in early development: A re-evaluation of the "play ethos".' In A. Pellegrini (ed) *Psychological Bases for Early Education*. London: John Wiley.

Sylva, K. and Lunt, I. (1980) *Child Development: A First Course.* Oxford: Basil Blackwell.

Sylva, K., Roy, C. and Painter, M. (1980) *Childwatching at Playgroup and Nursery School.* London: Grant McIntyre.

Thorne, B. (1993) *Gender Play: Girls and Boys in School.* Buckingham: Open University Press.

Tizard, B. and Hughes, M. (1984) *Young Children Learning: Talking and Thinking at Home and at School.* London: Fontana Paperbacks.

Trevarthen, C. (1980) 'The foundation of intersubjectivity: development of interpersonal and co-operative understanding in infants.' In D.R. Olson (ed) *The Foundations of Language and Thought.* New York: W.W.Norton and Co.

Wellman, H.M. (1990) *The Child's Theory of Mind.* Cambridge, Mass.: Bradford MIT.

Wells, G. (1987) *The Meaning Makers: Children Learning Language and Using Language to Learn.* London: Hodder and Stoughton.

Wood, D., McMahon, L. and Cranstoun, Y. (1980) *Working with Under Fives.* London: Grant McIntyre.

Woodhead, M. (1991) 'Psychology and the cultural construction of children's needs.' In M. Woodhead, P. Light and R. Carr. (eds) *Growing Up in a Changing Society.* Vol 3 of *Child Development in a Social Context.* London: Routledge.

CHAPTER SIX

Observation as a Tool for Assessment

For most people the word 'assessment' may well be associated with income tax assessments, or the rate at which insurance damages will have to be paid, or possibly the notion of assessment in the National Curriculum (the Standardised Assessment Tasks: SATS). Members of the teaching profession will undoubtedly have strong concepts of assessment, generally in terms of testing as a means of discovering what children have learned. Social workers' concept of assessment, however, will tend to mean weighing up the child's all-round development and problems with a view to taking decisions about possible action. Health workers in their medical context generally use the word in association with the monitoring of a child's developmental progress. While these several professional standpoints on the nature of assessment tend to overlap, each embodies a different way of thinking. The present chapter explores the relationship between observation and assessment in these various professional areas as well as touching on some practical aspects of assessment and the ways in which interdisciplinary 'case reviews' (a requirement of the Children Act) have brought all these professionals together.

The methods or tools which workers rely on for making assessments range from the very controlled and structured to the unintrusive and open-ended. Observation is one of these tools, coming at the informal end of the continuum, though it will probably contribute in some way to most other assessment procedures. This book has stressed throughout the importance of seeing what children are actually doing, hearing what they are actually saying, without as far as possible introducing preconceived ideas of what this might, or should, be. An open and receptive state of mind and an ability to record (mentally and on paper) the fine detail of a child's behaviour both involve skills and attitudes which have to be acquired. Non-interpretative, non-judgemental observation stands thus in sharp contrast to *assessment*, which is all about weighing up progress, judging what has been learned, interpreting behaviour, and making decisions. At the level of assessment-making the part played by personal expectations, value systems, cultural attitudes and professional priorities cannot be ignored. All these are inevitably present. No assessment can be purely objective and clinical. This problematic area is difficult to handle because such expectations, values and attitudes are often unconsciously held, and questioning deeply held beliefs can be uncomfortable and unsettling. In assessing children the problem must nevertheless be addressed. People who work with children will particularly need to consider their whole concept of childhood, their understanding of children's rights, and finally their attitudes to parents' own views about bringing up their children. In addition they need to be conscious of the framing effect of their own professional theory and ethos, which may help to direct thinking but could equally constrict it.

It is all too easy to jump to the conclusion that across the world people have similar ideas about small children. Comparisons of pre-schools in Japan, China and the USA reveal very different attitudes to pre-school children's behaviour and what constitutes a 'child-like' child (Tobin *et al.*, 1989). In one specific case, from Japan, four-year-old Hiroki spent an action-packed morning, noisily commenting on all his tasks, making jokes, singing loudly, interrupting other children, poking them, punching and wrestling. The assessments by pre-school professionals from the three countries interpreted his behaviour differently. Among the comments, an American regarded the child as intellectually gifted and easily bored. The Chinese thought he was spoiled. The Japanese, while recognising he was challenging to staff and children alike, remained unconcerned, the class teacher in fact considering it behaviour appropriate for his age. Another example, from Canada, contrasts the beliefs of First Nation tribal groups with typical North American practice. First Nation Elders valued collaboration and co-operation much more highly than the deeply held belief in the value of individuality typical of kindergarten teachers (Moss and Pence,1994; and Pence, 1995). This and many other insights are being gained through an innovative training programme, and associated pre-school provision, which is being developed collaboratively between members of First Nation tribal groups in Canada and the University of Victoria, British Columbia.

Adults working with children can generally be assumed to have positive motives for their work-choice but they probably rarely reflect on the power that they wield. Health and social workers may be more conscious of this as they make far-reaching proposals on a child's future, but even ordinary, everyday actions can have long-term consequences. Activities for groups of adults, either in the work place or on training courses, can be helpful in raising awareness about the issues of rights, reponsibilities and power. A collection of useful and imaginative activities for staff and students is given in Drummond et al., (1992). One of these activities also includes relevant sections from the 1989 UN Convention on the Rights of the Child.

The way that professional perspectives can shape judgements is nicely illustrated in this medical example. A radiologist's report of X-rays of a child with a persistent cough concluded that there was no apparent reason for the problem. However, a second radiograph showed a button in the child's throat. The button was removed and the cough stopped. The first X-ray was re-examined and the button was visible there too. The radiologist had too easily assumed that the child was wearing a vest with a button at the neck. Dr Jane Abercrombie, who used this case on training courses, points out that 'persistent, deep-rooted and well-organised classifications of ways of thinking and behaving' are always shaping our interpretations of situations or data (quoted in Drummond, 1993, p.79).

In the light of these warnings about the dangers of bias, narrow expectations, culture-bound perceptions and so on, it is helpful to set down guiding principles for all workers making assessments about young children. The insistence of the 1989 Children Act that the interests of the child are paramount must be the starting point. There must be respect for children as individuals, and for their personal experiences and achievements, and their cultural and religious backgrounds. Any assessment should recognise different learning and personal needs and take account of the child's view. Parents (or those standing in for them) should not feel excluded either. A reciprocal exchange of information with parents should always be incorporated into assessment arrangements. Readers will find more extensive discussions about the principles of assessment in Drummond et al. (1992), Drummond (1993) and Wolfendale (1993a and b). Whatever the work setting, principles will need to be agreed and made explicit before assessment procedures are adopted. The two should be logically connected.

The principles suggested above are relevant across all kinds of pre-school setting, but the assessment procedures typically associated with each have varied purposes and characteristics. This is the next topic for consideration.

Assessment in group settings for children under five (such as nursery schools and classes, playgroups, nurseries, and family or under-fives centres) may have as many as six different purposes: to learn about children as individuals; to monitor children's progress (or lack of it); to inform planning of the curriculum (all the activities, materials and organisational arrangements); to enable staff to evaluate the provision they offer; to gather information for communication to other professionals and parents; and to make the job more enjoyable (Lally and Hurst, 1992, p.72). The actual function of assessment varies according to the purpose. When focusing on an individual child's progress the emphasis will normally be on *formative* assessment, which is on-going and should give insight into areas such as learning, the child's feelings, and social relationships. Informed by this type of assessment adults are in a better position to plan appropriately for the individual child. For instance, with increased insight they may be able to judge whether the child is on the brink of a new phase of development, the 'zone of proximal development' as it was called by Vygotsky. Children learn most effectively and easily if adults are able to recognise and capitalise on this kind of 'readiness'. Formative assessment also aids planning for the group as a whole.

Diagnostic assessment is self-explanatory. It allows adults to identify areas of difficulty, where for instance a child needs special help or particular targeted activities. The importance of the pre-school years as a time for discovering special needs can hardly be over-emphasised. Diagnostic assessment based on observation spans all child-oriented services and professions, although in more general, non-specialised services staff are likely to refer to professionals outside their own service. The sensitive awareness and observations of staff will sometimes alert them to behaviour or symptoms which suggest problems in children's lives such as neglect or abuse (physical, emotional or sexual). Where there is concern on any score then staff will of course be expected to act quickly, making contact with appropriate local authority officers or other organisations, the NSPCC for example.

Another type of assessment is *summative*, which comes at the conclusion of a period. It *sums up* the progress and learning which have taken place. Final examinations at school and university are of this type, and so too are the Standardised Assessment Tasks or SATS. The intention behind SATS is to inform teachers and parents of what the children have achieved according to the kind of measure (in this case a test) which has been used. Such information does not, however, offer much insight into how children are thinking, nor can it shed any light on areas of learning other than those actually being examined. (An associated problem is that the pressure of testing may profoundly influence what is actually taught.) For various reasons summative assessment has least relevance at the pre-school stage. It frequently involves a test-type situation which is inappropriate for small children. Moreover, young children are so intensely curious that they are very easily distracted by something which seems more interesting. As a result they may well not concentrate on the test or task they are being set or may become fascinated by some irrelevant aspect of it. They are in addition very sensitive to the social context. Their ease with people they know contrasts often with wariness and shyness in the presence of an unfamiliar person. But even a known adult behaving in an unfamiliar manner can be disconcerting. The child's interpretation of the setting is also very influential on their response. Donaldson (1978) and Tizard and Hughes (1984) describe the variations in children's understanding and in their responses to situations. Donaldson has explored children's thinking in Piagetian tasks. Her imaginative re-casting of these tasks and her attention to children's knowledge of context have shed fresh light on children's stages of understanding. Thus, to find out about children's understanding of space and perspective, one of the tasks involves a boy trying to hide behind certain walls so that the 'policeman' could not see him. This was an improvement on Piaget's Swiss original which was based on the visibility of mountains behind various other hills and perhaps failed to allow for the likelihood that Swiss children more familiar with mountains might make sense of this task at an earlier age than those used to cities or flatter landscapes.

Evaluative assessment may not be centred on a single child, even though observation of individual children will still contribute to this kind of assessment. The goal of evaluation is to 'weigh up' the quality of what is being offered in terms of equipment, activities, the contributions of the staff, and the environment in general. Sometimes the word 'review' is employed to mean evaluation of this type. The Time Sampling example given earlier (in Chapter Four, *Observational Methods and Practice*) paid attention to the use of the book corner. Information recorded in this observation would therefore count as evaluative. Which children were observed in the book corner? How often were they there? What were they actually doing? Based on such evaluative assessment the book corner might be re-designed. Alternative ways of organising the space might emerge, or of improving the collection and use of the books.

Drummond (1993) includes one other type of assessment, which she labels *informative* and which specially concerns the reciprocal sharing of information about children between parents and pre-school staff. This matters because parents are the first 'educators' of their children and should be seen as partners by pre-school workers. The Children Act promotes the idea of partnership with parents, and most services for young children try to realise this with varying degrees of intensity and success. Partnership is a broad concept and the comments that follow deal only with the sharing of information in that relationship. Since parents want (and have a right) to know how their child is getting on, pre-school staff need ways of collecting and communicating this information – in other words they require a record-keeping system. In developing an effective system the following criteria are worth bearing in mind. Whichever one is chosen it must be easy to use and understood by other workers and parents; it must be precise and as quick to complete as possible; and the information it brings together must be factual and not based on interpretations and assumptions. Many different record-keeping systems are to be found in use. Some relate to a curriculum approach like High/Scope in which the record – called a Child Anecdotal Record (CAR) – is based on the 'Key Experiences' (which include language, number, shape and time). Other systems have different origins. 'Playladders' was developed for children with special educational needs, but has since been adapted for other children. Another system requires parents to fill in the details in a booklet, *All About Me* (Wolfendale, 1990), with the aim of presenting a lively and unique picture of a child's competencies at home. The seven areas emphasised here are: language; playing and learning; doing things for myself; my physical development; my health and and my habits; other people and how I behave; my moods and feelings. (More information about these and other systems is given in Drummond *et al.*, 1992.) In addition many pre-school groups keep, for each child, a portfolio (or file) in which are placed items selected by either the child or the adults. Typical portfolios would include drawings, paintings, perhaps photographs and other two-dimensional work, and observations by the staff. Material from informative assessments may be passed on to the next pre-school group, or to statutory school.

As children enter school they may well be screened by some form of 'base-line assessment'. The purposes are to help curriculum planning, to provide a baseline against which later achievements can be measured, and to help identify special needs. This assessment is somewhat controversial and can be criticised using the arguments that might be deployed against any pre-school testing. Certainly it is undesirable that teachers are required to spend much time administering such assessments, time which would be better spent in more active involvement with children and teaching. All the same, teachers and local education authorities may be pressured into accepting this development in order to safeguard themselves, for at least it allows them to demonstrate what the children were capable of on entry to school when compared with what they achieve in Key Stage 1 testing at the age of seven. Wolfendale has investigated this dilemma and reported her findings in a booklet published by OMEP (1993a).

One of the consequences of the increasing partnership and collaboration between different services, voluntary organisations and parents, which is evolving in the wake of the Children Act, is the need for workers to clarify their meaning of key words. With colleagues in our everyday work places we use jargon and short cuts in our language. There is nothing wrong with this; indeed it speeds up communication. Inter-disciplinary dialogue, however, must necessarily be at a more explicit level, free from possible ambiguities. Discussion about terminology is often rewarding and revealing, for it helps to clarify personal understanding. 'Assessment' is one of these key words which may need clarification. As pointed out already, it has various shades of meaning, and sometimes benefits from an accompanying adjective, such as 'diagnostic' or 'normative'.

Social workers use the word 'assessment' in a slightly different way from those so far discussed. The link between observation and assessment is also rather different. The social worker's role with regard to children is clearly a specialised one. It applies largely to the protection of children vulnerable in some way and to the promotion of positive health and all-round development. In social work the term assessment is most commonly used to describe the stage at which a range of information is brought together with the purpose of making plans for the child's future. Nevertheless, there is a stage before this when the term might also be found, namely at the warning and referral level. Observation is a very important tool at this point. An alert, well-trained social worker will be able to recognise signs that children's physical health and development are being impaired or are likely to be damaged as a consequence of the care (or lack of it) they are receiving. The same applies to their mental health. The Children Act has been criticised for its terminology – especially its use of words such as 'need' and 'health' – since these are relative, not absolute, terms. Elsewhere the Act lays stress on taking account of class and cultural diversity, but it is very difficult for professionals to make sensible decisions about more marginal cases or cases involving contexts far removed from their own experience. In addition to recognising health and development problems, social workers, and indeed all workers with young children, should be on the look out for symptoms which may indicate stress, neglect or abuse. Some of these have already been mentioned earlier in this book, but it is worth repeating them here. Workers should note children who are withdrawn, 'frozen', or excessively watchful; who seem unable to enjoy themselves, miserable and anxious; who are hostile and behave angrily; who have a very low tolerance of frustration or failure (judged according to their age); who have difficulty with new situations; who have poor relationships with other children and adults; and who exhibit low self-esteem. The assessment of children in need (and the Act in general) is usefully covered in *Working with Children and the Children Act* (Herbert, 1993).

The new 'Competences' used in social work (CCETSW, 1995) include the category *assess and plan* – where assessment implies bringing together information from various sources for review. Partnership is an essential element in this process of gathering and reviewing information. The types of evidence needed will include observations made by any adults involved with the child (carers, health workers, and parents as well as social workers). Other forms of evidence may include interviews with children or material from play sessions (see Garbarino *et al.*, 1989) which enable adults to discover, among other things, children's wishes and feelings (a Children Act requirement). Observations may also give insights into the emotional states and attitudes of the children. In making a comprehensive assessment much more information will be needed regarding not only the child, but the family too in its ecological situation and in regard to its possible network of relationships (including friends and neighbourhood supports). All this will be pieced together from many sources, including any workers (professional and voluntary) who have connections with the child and her/his family.

Assessing Outcomes in Child Care is the title given to the *Looking After Children* project report (Parker *et al.*, 1991). Assessment here refers to a scheme for monitoring children from birth to eighteen who are being 'looked after' away from their birth parents. The schedules from this comprehensive, interprofessional project are being widely used by local authorities. The project is also seen as a general model for use in monitoring children's progress. It covers seven 'dimensions': Health, Education, Emotional and Behavioural Development, Family and Peer Relationships, Self-care and Competence, Identity, and Social Presentation. Not all these dimensions have the same emphasis at each age. For example the final one, Social Presentation, is especially relevant from puberty onwards. The project members believe that while birth parents are usually knowledgeable about their children across all these dimensions (absorbing information often subconsciously), social services departments responsible for bringing up children cannot leave the collection of facts to chance. There has to be a systematic way of gathering, recording and using the data. *Looking After Children* has tried to avoid a simplistic checklist approach and has designed a structure which enables a broad and comprehensive picture of the child's progress to evolve. Health service staff, carers, teachers and other workers connected with the child will all take part in the case review when the schedules in all dimensions are completed or updated. Their contributions will often be based on observation.

In the social work context, whether at the early stage of recognising that a problem exists (that a child may be 'in need' or 'at risk'), at the investigative stage of gathering information, during the assessment of the case leading to decision-making, and in the later phases of reviewing and monitoring progress, observation will almost always play a part. At every stage the skilled observer will take time to watch and listen, to remain calm and thoughtful and, most importantly, to avoid rushing to conclusions too rapidly.

References and further reading

Blenkin, G.M. and Kelly, A.V. (1992) *Assessment in Early Childhood Education.* London: Paul Chapman Publishing.

CCETSW (1995) *Rules and Requirements for the Diploma in Social Work.* London: Central Council for Education and Training of Social Workers.

Donaldson, M. (1978) *Children's Minds.* London: Croom Helm.

Drummond, M.J., Rouse, D. and Pugh, G. (1992) *Making Assessment Work: Values and Principles in Assessing Children's Learning.* (A training pack) London: NES/National Children's Bureau.

Drummond, M.J. (1993) *Assessing Children's Learning.* London: David Fulton.

Garbarino, J., Stott, F.M. and the Faculty of the Erickson Institute (1989) *What Children Can Tell Us: Eliciting, Interpreting and Evaluating Information from Children.* San Francisco: Jossey-Bass Publishers.

Herbert, M. (1993) *Working with Children and the Children Act.* London: British Psychological Society.

Lally, M. and Hurst, V. (1992) 'Assessment in nursery education: A review of approaches.' In G.M. Blenkin and A.V. Kelly (eds) *Assessment in Early Childhood Education.* London: Paul Chapman Publishing.

Moss, P. and Pence, A. (1994) *Valuing Quality.* London: Paul Chapman Publishing.

Parker, R., Ward, H., Jackson, S., Aldgate, J. and Wedge, P. (1991) *Assessing Outcomes in Child Care.* The Report of an Independent Working Party established by the Department of Health. (The Looking After Children Project.) London: HMSO.

Pence, A. (1995) *Making Change Happen: the Integration of Care and Education.* Seminar at the Institute of Education, University of London.

Phillips, M. for the Department of Health (1988) *Protecting Children: A Guide for Social Workers undertaking a Comprehensive Assessment.* London: HMSO.

Tizard, B. and Hughes, M. (1984) *Young Children Learning: Talking and Thinking at Home and at School.* London: Fontana.

Tobin, J.J., David, Y.H. and Davidson, D.H. (1989) *Preschool in Three Cultures.* New Haven and London: Yale University Press

Wolfendale, S. (1990) *All About Me.* Nottingham: NES/Arnold.

Wolfendale, S. (1993a) *Baseline Assessment: A Review of Current Practice, Issues and Strategies for Effective Implementation.* London: OMEP (UK).

Wolfendale, S. (1993b) *Assessing Special Educational Needs.* London: Cassell.

CHAPTER SEVEN

Teaching Child Observation

This chapter primarily addresses lecturers designing course programmes that cover the topic of child observation. Much of the material it contains has been inspired by personal experience, as well as by a pilot project initiated by CCETSW (Central Council for Education and Training of Social Workers) to explore ways of teaching child observation on Diploma in Social Work course programmes. While what follows should ideally suit courses in all disciplines, it must be acknowledged that it is biased towards the training of social workers since there is a dearth of appropriate literature for this particular group. But there will still be much that is applicable to any course organiser, especially those working with more mature students.

The first part of the chapter identifies the learning objectives for course programmes, while the second part sets out various strategies for achieving these, notably through lectures, seminars, observation sessions, analysis, evaluation and assessment. The final section addresses general issues about course design and timetabling.

Learning objectives

Lecturers intending to introduce planned child observation on pre-service training programmes will need to be fully convinced and clear about the value of such sessions. The pressures of an already over-crowded syllabus and the notion that child observation is a worthy, but minority, interest, will particularly have to be resisted. The achievement of many of the new Competences outlined in the revised Rules and Requirements for the Diploma in Social Work (CCETSW, 1995) depends, however, on observational skills. The most obviously related Competences are: *communicate and engage, promote and enable, assess and plan,* and *intervene and provide services.* Chapter One of this book set out to explain why observation matters and covered the rationale in some detail. These ideas will now be presented in the form of learning objectives for courses.

By the end of their course programme students should have knowledge of the purposes and methods of several observation techniques, and should be able to put one or two into practice and evaluate the processes involved. They should understand that alternative techniques allow totally different data to be collected (see Chapter Four) and that each has different merits and limitations. Learning how to make observational records is to a large extent a matter of skill development, and therefore needs practice, but it also requires a knowledge of methods, an understanding of the problems of objectivity and the use of critical judgement in evaluation. The skills of observation contrast markedly with the active intervention which is typical of social workers' roles (and those of other professionals working with children). Students need to be initiated into this seemingly passive mode of behaviour, which they may feel is almost unnatural. They must learn to adopt and maintain a heightened, focussed state of attention in which they see and hear as much as possible. They must learn that it is only through this intense, absorbed watching that they can acquire detailed information about behaviour and development.

Skilled observers understand how discrimination operates and how it relates to observation. They will be well-informed about and alive to differences not only of race, culture and gender, but also of class, disability and sexual orientation. This awareness will be evident at two levels: knowledge at a personal level (recognising where prejudice and stereotyping exist in oneself), and knowledge of sources of discrimination within society (and how these may be structurally present in pre-school services and in the lives of some children). Children's rights and points-of-view in a potentially oppressive hierarchy need to be acknowledged.

Learning about child development is often associated with child observation, a logical connection. All social work students are required to be familiar with the milestones of development, and this knowledge should be brought together in a holistic view of the child's growth (see Chapter Five). When learning about the factors which promote good, all-round development (another CCETSW requirement), an ecological perspective is essential (as explained in Chapter Two).

The seminars and observations may also give students the opportunity to consider how they use themselves and their past experiences as they learn about children and their lives. Finally, students must appreciate that observation is simply the first stage in a process of gathering fundamental information to serve as the basis for assessments and plans for intervention (the topic of Chapter Six).

In summary, there are general observational skills and associated learning which are applicable and transferable across many professional settings and age ranges, but in addition there are skills and a body of knowledge which relate more specifically to children.

Teaching observation skills

Although there is a place for introductory lectures, the skills of observation will be best developed through experiential learning. The following pattern is suggested: an introductory lecture, preparatory activities in seminar groups (of not more than ten), a series of observational visits, and then further seminars at which students make presentations of their observations and discuss issues of interest or concern.

Having outlined the rationale of observation the preparatory lecture and seminars should introduce students to some of the possible recording strategies (set out in Chapter Four) and provide opportunities to experiment with these, thereby discovering their possibilities. The material for these activities can be either brief video sequences or simple, short, role plays. Almost any section of video showing children interacting might be used, although one with a distracting voice-over commentary is not recommended. By having the whole group watch it together and recording at the same time what they have observed, several other topics may be explored in addition to the recording method itself. One significant topic to highlight in this way is that of subjectivity. Even experienced professionals are often less objective, dispassionate and distanced than they assume. (Certainly the CCETSW pilot project members were shocked when they discovered the power of their own experiences and views in circumscribing their perceptions.) A very ordinary sample of behaviour may be seen very differently by different observers, and it is worthwhile 'engineering' such a contrast of views in a seminar to make the point vividly. Students might thus be shown a section of video *after* being prepared with different pre-information: one half of the group might be told (without the others hearing) that they are about to see an ordinary family scene, while the rest are informed that there is a suspicion of abuse. The subsequent perceptions of the two groups are likely to be strikingly at odds.

Students' interpretations and feelings about behaviour may relate back to their own childhood. A comparison of family rules or attitudes would bring this topic into focus. Outside the planned observation task students might be able to visit each other on placement in order to compare their immediate impressions as a visitor with the perceptions of the student on the spot who has become familiar with the scene and atmosphere.

In addition to the inevitable subjectivity of observation, the question of selectivity arises in recording just what is observed. Everything cannot be written down; choices must be made. This can be demonstrated by getting students to compare their notes of a shared observation in a seminar.

The role of memory, selectivity and subjectivity might be analysed following an experiment with 'process recording' (Ford and Jones, 1987). The practice of this technique (quite commonly used in social work) involves the participant writing a chronological account, from memory, of a short role play, describing what took place, why they reacted as they did in their role, how they interpreted the responses of the other participants, and finally what in retrospect they learned from the episode emotionally and otherwise.

Other activities valuable in raising awareness of individual perceptions are suggested in Drummond *et al.* (1992), who provide, for example, a set of photographs which can be photocopied and used to trigger spontaneous discussion from students. Among the set are photographs which should elicit discussion about sexist and racist attitudes. The issue of stereotyping on the basis of class, culture, race, gender, sexual orientation and disability should be reviewed at this stage, before the actual observations take place. No-one can escape absorbing values and attitudes, some of which will undoubtedly be negative. Full awareness of the risk of these influencing observation is therefore vital. Group members might also be asked to empathise with those who suffer discrimination by sharing personal experiences of unfairness, or of situations when others have misinterpreted their intentions.

When practising observation techniques and making comparisons the nature of the vocabulary used can be highlighted. Students have to learn to use *descriptive* language, not *judgemental* or *interpretative* language. For example:

Descriptive:	'Places bricks on table noisily'
Judgemental:	'Places bricks on table in an angry manner'
Interpretative:	'Shows he's tired and in a bad mood to-day as he places bricks on table'

Preparation for a child study involves helping students in the process of selecting a suitable child to observe. When such a study is part of a social work placement, students should be advised not to choose a child identified as needing special intervention, for this raises ethical issues. Where vulnerable people are concerned, close scrutiny by an observer might be intrusive and even harmful, placing additional strain on children who may be 'at risk', 'in need', or facing other difficulties in their lives. Furthermore it is better for students not to be involved in the continuing assessment procedures surrounding such children, but to concentrate entirely on learning the skills of observation.

The actual setting up of the observational visits might seem time-consuming, but it will be time well-spent. Students should always select a child who is unknown to them (another reason for students on social work placement not to choose one of their client cases). It is best to find a subject by making contact with an ordinary pre-school group – a playgroup, parent and toddler group, a nursery school or nursery class or private nursery – rather than a social services day nursery or family centre. (For more information about settings see Chapter Three.) Most students seem to find their own pre-school group without much difficulty, but it may be helpful for the tutor to compile a list of local groups which have been welcoming in the past and issue this to students if necessary. The task of investigating pre-school resources and making contact is relevant experience in relation to the new social work Competences. Students will require a letter of introduction from the university or college which explains the nature of the child study observations, why the student has been asked to do them, how many visits they will make, and what is expected of the pre-school staff. A detailed account of the process of making contact and negotiating the arrangement will be found in the second half of Chapter Four. It is vital that the students make clear to pre-school leaders what they will be doing and why. In these ways the Competences of *communicating and engaging* (forming relationships and explaining a task) and *promoting and enabling*, as well as *assessing and planning* (in particular learning about other professionals and the voluntary services), are all featured.

At the planning stage lecturers should also advise students as to what to do if they observe situations which seem dangerous or damaging to children. Though a student observer would normally only intervene, as any concerned citizen would, if a child was in imminent physical danger, there may be other worrying aspects (such as inadequate child care, racism, sexism or other forms of discrimination) which it would not be appropriate for the student to raise with the staff. These matters must, however, be discussed with the lecturer as soon as possible.

Frequently observation triggers childhood memories, both positive or disturbing. At the start of the preparatory seminars it is advisable to remind the students of the support systems they have access to in their institution (counselling services, tutorial support, specific support networks, etc.). The matter of personal disclosure is best raised at this point so that members of the seminar group can control the extent to which they share their past or present feelings. In any case, the emphasis of the seminars is on the development of observation skills. The seminars are not an appropriate forum for counselling.

Once the observational visits are under way, seminar groups are valuable for support, for discussion of issues arising from the observations and for student presentations. There will need to be properly established ground rules regarding confidentiality. Students must at all times ensure the anonymity of their subjects and settings.

Some course leaders will wish to take the opportunity to examine theoretical perspectives in relation to the observations made by the students. Such theories may form the focus of seminar discussions, or be required in the writing up of a child study. Lectures and/or reading will have introduced the students to the principal theories and placed these theories in their context of time, place and ideological standpoint. Chapters Two and Five have introduced a selection of theoretical views of relevance in the study of young children. Potentially valuable is critical reflection on student observations in the light of different theories, since these offer a framework in which fragmentary observations may be located and also help to explain what was recorded. Students must of course be encouraged to be sceptical and independent in their thinking. Should their observations seem to refute the apparent wisdom of the theory they should be encouraged to debate the matter. They may need to be reminded of course that they have studied only one child and should be wary of generalising from such limited evidence. Every child is unique and cannot stand as representative of all the others.

Towards the end of the seminars it is valuable for tutors to encourage students to reflect on themselves as observers. The planned observations can be reviewed by prompting discussion on what has been learned, and what has been enjoyed. Negative aspects should not be ignored – such as recognising whether the observers found themselves making assumptions and labelling children, having limited ideas about what children should do, or recognising that they have been driven by a single theoretical perspective. The impact that the observational visits have had on all concerned should also be explored at this stage. The last part of Chapter Four looks at all the various groups of people in turn, children, parents, pre-school staff and observers.

Possible models for child observation on social work course programmes

For course tutors having to face the practicalities of incorporating child observation within course programmes, there are several problems to overcome. Given the pressure of an already over-stretched curriculum, the most significant is how best to fit in a meaningful series of planned observations with associated seminars. What is the minimum number of observations and seminars which is practically viable, and will this at the same time give students sufficient time for worthwhile learning? A second difficulty lies in finding appropriate staff to lead the seminars, and a third in deciding the ideological framework (if any) in which the observations should be located. Guidance for social work course programmes (CCETSW, 1991) includes a chapter on child observation. This sets out the rationale and identifies the special skills that students acquire from the experience of observation. It advocates the 'Tavistock' method (outlined in Chapter Four of this book) which requires an extensive amount of time devoted to it – typically fifteen separate hour-long observations, plus weekly seminars at which students present their observations. The CCETSW guidelines suggest that the actual aims of observation are to record: '(a) the interaction that has been observed; (b) the emotional state (mood) of those observed as perceived by the observer; (c) the observer's own reponse to the situation' (CCETSW, 1991, p.132). This approach to observation is therefore essentially psychoanalytical. Several examples of the basic model are mentioned in the guidelines. A further account (McMahon and Farnfield, 1994) describes in more detail an actual course at the University of Reading. Around the country other institutions'are experimenting with somewhat different models, and the pilot project in the South West was part of this search to find an alternative way of addressing the various problems.

The University of Bristol model described below is a compromise, not an ideal. It has been designed to suit existing structures within a given institution and to draw as far as possible on staff already available (although it is necessary sometimes to bring in colleagues who are skilled in the field of child care). It takes an eclectic line towards theory but pays particular attention to the ecology of human development. The Diploma in Social Work course programme uses an Enquiry and Action Learning (EAL) method (Burgess and Jackson, 1990), so to a large extent it is based on case-studies using problem-solving methods in experiential, collaborative group work The seventy or so students per year are divided into 'study groups' of ten students, each group having a tutor as 'facilitator'. Ten to a group is a maximum, and eight would be better. Bristol's DipSW programme has in fact long included a study of a pre-school child, although the actual format has been modified with changing circumstances. Currently this study is located in the first term of the programme, and is required of all students whatever their specialist interest. It is no longer associated with a practice placement. The child study seminars take place in the study groups already formed as the usual work setting of their university course. Where the facilitator does not have experience in the field of child care (and/or observation), other colleagues, from within or outside the university, are drafted in. It is preferable for all tutors themselves to have carried out a child study and participated in related seminars.

On this course programme the child study is founded on observational visits. It aims to develop the skills of observation, to increase awareness of children's development and behaviour through observation and theoretical insights, and finally to teach students how to evaluate the observational process. Students attend lectures on child development in the same term as they carry out their observations. These lectures attempt to give an overview of the subject and its different theoretical standpoints.

The child study depends on a series of observations of a pre-school child (aged between eighteen months and four years) in both a group setting and the child's home. The preliminary visit to a pre-school group is the occasion for setting up the arrangements, seeking the help of the group leader in the selection of a child for observation and making plans for contacting the parents. Students take their letter of introduction with them on this visit and explain carefully the reasons for the study and how they propose to carry out their observations. Bristol requires students to make a minimum of three visits to the pre-school group and one to the child's home. Each observation must last not less than thirty minutes and is preceded by approximately fifteen minutes tuning in to the group environment. The reason for including a home visit is to help the students gain a more rounded picture of their study child's behaviour, to consider the broader ecology of the child's life, and to learn something of the parents' viewpoints. Tutors should always emphasise to students that visits are not judgemental and that parents should feel that the student is interested in their child for the sake of their studies.

All observational visits must be properly recorded, on the spot. These records become the source data for a written assignment and might also be used for presentations in study groups. The written assignment is an assessed piece of work. Although some social work tutors believe that observational studies ought not to be used in this way, having the exercise properly assessed demonstrates that it is a serious and integral part of the course. In writing up their child study, students must present their observations, evaluate the observational process, examine one or two aspects of child development (drawing on their reading) and also demonstrate their understanding of anti-discriminatory issues.

Tutors are well aware that the series of observational visits is all too brief, but since it is clear that most students learn a great deal from them, find the child study task interesting, rewarding and often enjoyable, it is worthwhile continuing.

In some institutions the study of an Area of Particular Practice (APP), in the second year of the DipSW programme, includes a more extensive observational project, and at this stage it is appropriate to give attention to the assessment of children's needs.

Conclusion

The observation of young children's complex and rapid development is a rich and fascinating activity. Close attention to the detail of their play, interactions, relationships and learning, often brings surprises and certainly rewards to the observer. Once having learned the skills of observation – how to remain inconspicuous, motivated and able to sustain attention without 'switching off', recognising the selectivity of any observation, as well as being alert to potential biases and assumptions –

the observer can transfer these skills to many situations and to people of all ages. Indeed, skilled observation can become a way of life.

References and further reading

Burgess, H. and Jackson, S. (1990) 'Enquiry and action learning: A new approach to social work education.' *Social Work Education 9*, 3.

CCETSW (1991) *The Teaching of Child Care in the Diploma in Social Work.* London: CCETSW.

CCETSW (1995) *Rules and Requirements for the Diploma in Social Work (Revised edition of Paper 30).* London: CCETSW.

Drummond, M.J., Rouse, D. and Pugh, G. (1992) *Making Assessment Work: Values and Principles in Assessing Children's Learning.* London: National Children's Bureau.

Ford, K. and Jones, A. (1987) *Student Supervision.* London: BASW/MacMillan.

McMahon, L. and Farnfield, S. (1994) 'Infant and child observation as preparation for social work practice.' *Social Work Education 13*, 3.

The TASK Code Categories

The Target Child method has a column labelled *TASK* which refers to the kind of activity the child is engaged in. These activities may consist of a particular task or type of play but the list below also includes non-play and other ways a child may be spending the time.

Large muscle movement – LMM: Active movement, such as climbing, running, jumping, using the larger muscles.

Large-scale construction – LSC: Building with planks, PVC covered soft blocks, big boxes and bricks etc.

Small-scale construction – SSC: Using small-scale constructional materials such as Lego, Mobilo and Sticklebricks.

Scale-version toys – SVT: Organising small-scale objects such as toy cars, zoo or farm animals. If the toys are being used in pretend play, use the next category.

Pretend – PRE: Using objects 'as if' they are something else. Sometimes called imaginative play.

Structured materials – SM: Using materials with a particular purpose, e.g. jigsaw puzzles, peg-boards, shape posting boxes, bead-threading.

Art – ART: Drawing, painting, cutting and sticking.

Manipulation – MAN: Mastering or refining skills which require hand and eye co-ordination, e.g. handling sand, dough, clay, water, etc. Also sewing and gardening.

Adult-directed craft and manipulation – ADM: Adults guiding and directing children (sometimes with an adult-determined end product) e.g. in the making of festive cards, tracing, directed collage, etc.

Three Rs Activities – 3Rs: Making attempts at reading, writing or counting.

Examination – EX: Examining an object or material with care, e.g. looking through a magnifying glass.

Problem-solving – PS: Trying to solve a problem in a logical way, e.g. looking to see why something will not work and trying to put it right.

Games with rules – GWR: Playing ball games, circle and singing games, board games such as lotto and snakes and ladders.

Informal games – IG: Playing spontaneously, e.g. loosely organised games between two or more children, following each other around, chanting, holding hands and jumping.

Music – MUS: Listening to any kind of music, playing instruments, singing as a group or alone.

Passive adult-led group activities – PALGA: Adult leading a large group of children, e.g. stories, finger rhymes, watching television, or demonstrating (e.g. how to plant seeds).

Social interaction, non-play – SINP: This category is used only when a child is not engaged in any of the other task code categories. It covers social interaction with another child or adult, verbal or non-verbal, e.g. chatting, seeking help, teasing, being comforted by an adult.

Distress behaviour – DB: The child is visibly distressed and seeking comfort or attention from an adult or a child.

Standing around, aimless wander or gaze – SA/AWG: The child is not actively engaged in a task or watching something specific.

Roaming – RO: 'Butterfly' behaviour, the child appears to be searching for something to do.

Purposeful movement – PM: The child moves with deliberate intention towards a person, place or object, e.g. looking for a piece of equipment, going outdoors.

Waiting – W: The child is inactive, waiting for an adult or child.

Watching – WA: The child is watching other people or events, listening in to conversations, but not participating.

Domestic activity – DA: This category includes going to the toilet, hand-washing, arriving and departing, snacks and meals.

(The above categories have been adapted from Sylva, K., Roy, C. and Painter, M. (1980) *Childwatching at Playgroup and Nursery School.* London: Grant McIntyre. pp.240–243.)